SHED
MANUAL

Designing, building and fitting out your perfect shed

First published in April 2019

British Library Cataloguing in Publication Data
A catalogue record for this book is available from
the British Library.

ISBN 978 1 78521 220 8

Library of Congress control no: 2018938912

Published by Haynes Publishing,
Sparkford, Yeovil, Somerset BA22 7JJ, UK
Tel: 01963 440635
Int. tel: +44 1963 440635
Website: www.haynes.com

Haynes North America Inc.
859 Lawrence Drive, Newbury Park,
California 91320, USA

Printed in Malaysia

SHED
MANUAL

Designing, building and fitting out your perfect shed

John Coupe and Alex Johnson

Contents

INTRODUCTION

◄ Shingles on a shed: How to make your own. (Cuprinol Shed of the Year)

Everybody wants their own hideaway. And the best is the one you build yourself.

As children, we stretch sheets between chairs, turn huge cardboard boxes into dens and make satisfyingly unsafe lean-tos with branches in woods. My parents helped me to make my first shed aged seven, using bits of old unwanted wood by the side of the garage and the back of an old bookcase. That love of constructing our own little refuge does not diminish with time. In adulthood, there is still a strong urge to build sheds for storage, shelter, or simply somewhere to escape the everyday world.

The idea of the shed as the basic building block of all structures goes back millennia. The ancient Roman engineer Vitruvius wrote that a building should have 'firmitas', 'utilitas' and 'venustas' – in other words, it should stand up, it should be fit for purpose and it should look good. These are all key aspects of shed building, as the following pages will show. As the American architect and theorist Robert Venturi puts it, all architects do is make 'decorated sheds'.

There have been buildings in gardens around the world for thousands of years. In China, pavilions were built at least as early as the Zhou dynasty (1122 to 256 BC), while in AD 61 to c.112, well-to-do Romans like Pliny the Younger ('When I retire to this garden summerhouse, I fancy myself a hundred miles away from my villa') were keen on embellishing their gardens with a range of temples, nymphaeums – a type of watery grotto – and monuments. The Emperor Hadrian's villa at Tivoli had around 60 different garden buildings. In Japan, traditional wooden tea houses became popular during the Sengoku period, between the 15th and 17th centuries. These were built by Zen monks searching for somewhere simple and tranquil, embodying the Japanese concept of wabi-sabi, attractive transience.

The word 'shed' goes back hundreds of years. In Anglo-Saxon English, it seems to be linked to the idea of shade or protection from the elements, as well as the notion of something separate that was also covered. And that's how we commonly picture it today – a typical shed is a straightforward roofed building, usually with one room, one storey and probably at least one window, mostly found in back gardens and allotments (if it's not on the ground, it morphs into a 'treehouse'). Size can vary – though once a shed gets too large it starts to edge towards 'barn' or 'stable' territory – and even the humblest sheds may include features such as electrics and solar panels.

Sheds can be made out of anything. In 1960, Alfred Heineken visited the island of Curaçao and noticed: a) that there was a housing shortage and b) that there were empty beer bottles scattered everywhere. So, in an impressive lightbulb moment, he asked architect John Habraken to design him a bottle that could also be used as a brick. The

▶ The Woodland Stargazer: Garden sheds can be any shape or size. (Cuprinol Shed of the Year)

results were special bricks known as WOBOs (WOrld BOttles), which were used to build a shed on the Heineken estate. Only 1,000 'bricks' were needed to build a basic 10 x 10ft shed.

One of the beauties of doing it yourself is that you can pick whatever building materials you choose for your shed. Cob, for example, is a very old building material that combines earth, straw, sand and water in a sturdy way to form lumps or 'cobs' which you then press together to form walls up to two feet thick with impressive thermal capabilities. Plastic and metal sheds are also common, but despite their durable qualities the most widely used material is wood, partly because of its pleasing aesthetic feel in a garden but also because most people are more familiar with working with wood.

You can use a shed for almost anything. At its simplest level, a shed is a storage space, whether that's for tools or other more general items. A shed on an allotment can house a vast number of useful bits and pieces, as well as providing a sheltered space for a cup of tea and a couple of chairs. It can also house specific items such as bicycles, in which case it will be sized appropriately.

Larger sheds and summerhouses – not to mention beach

▲▼ 'She Sheds' for women are increasingly popular, catering for all ages and tastes.

huts – are also perfect places to carry out hobbies or simply to use for relaxing. In more recent years, they have also become home to growing numbers of people working from home. One of the most famous shedworkers was playwright George Bernard Shaw, who wrote *Pygmalion* and *Major*

Barbara in a shed built in 1906 with a revolving base. This writing refuge, at his home in Shaw's Corner, Ayot St Lawrence, Hertfordshire, could thus be moved to improve the light or change the view.

Indeed, there are many variations on the basic shed model. Shepherds' huts have undergone a significant renaissance in the last decade, while a quick look at the entries for the annual Shed of the Year competition shows ingenious 'sheddies' at work at everything from eco summerhouses to Tardis replicas. There is even a special section for pub sheds. And bringing the shed story right up to date is the growing tiny house movement, which has taken the idea of living small to its ultimate shedlike conclusion.

Sheds are so engrained in our culture that they also play an important part in our health provision. The Men's Sheds movement was established in Australia in 2006 to provide local venues in which men – often of retirement age – can meet, socialise and work on practical tasks on a regular basis with other local men (see page 172 for more details). Since then, the concept has caught on elsewhere, and the first Men's Shed Association opened in England in 2009 – the latest figures from the UK Men's Sheds Association shows that more than 450 are now active.

Whatever you want to do with your shed and whether you've built one before or are contemplating your first attempt, this book will show you exactly how to go about it.

▼ George Bernard Shaw's writing hut.

Case study: Bonny Landsborough (@LottieShed)

I'm 65 and had never done anything like this in my life, but I just thought go on, do it, have a go! And I'm so pleased that I did do it. I love it. It has holes in it, some deliberate and some not. The sparrows roost in it at night and last spring a wren made a nest in it! I did it all on my own using bits of wood to prop up the walls while I nailed them in place. I only used hand tools. I haven't got any power tools, so it was hard work. It cost me £30 for the roof and nails.

The first shed I got years ago was a regular one bought from Homebase, but I have always wanted to build my own in the tradition of old allotmenteers. My friends were all amazed, but I told them it was only like making a dress – cut pieces to size and fix them together. I'm thinking of extending it to include a bird hide!

It's a small 6 x 4, on my allotment, made from scrap wood and corrugated metal found in skips and on the allotment site. Someone gave me an old children's play house and I raised the sides and put a new roof on it. I needed more storage space. I already have one small hut (a bought one), but it was full to bursting with gardening equipment.

I've put up shelves and made the odd bird box, but that is the limit of my skills! The hardest thing to do was work out how to make the base – i.e. dig posts into the ground or free standing on top of slabs. I chose the latter. Also I did it all on my own, when having an extra pair of hands would have been good. But then I'm like that – if I want to do something I just do it rather than wait for help!

Nothing really went wrong. It has got holes in it, it's not 'perfect', but then I wasn't aiming for perfect. I wanted a real old-fashioned allotment shed. It's got a strong frame and is actually very sturdy.

GETTING STARTED

Before we crack on with the details of the tools, materials, parts and components you will need to build a shed, let's just take a minute or two to cover a couple of very important – but not so immediately interesting – points. These will ensure that what you build complies with local and national regulations, and also that you finish the project as fit and healthy as you started it.

If you ignore local planning and building regulations it is possible that you will be asked to dismantle and move your lovingly crafted new building. Reading the following section will help you understand the regulations and the finer details that apply where you live.

Building a shed involves many operations. If not thought through correctly, these can be hazardous to both your health and the health of those working with you. Many books have been written on Health and Safety, but this introduction will highlight the issues that you need to consider as your plans progress from idea through to completion. The first issue is to make sure that your new building will comply with local rules and regulations.

Planning and building control

Planning and building control applies to most residential areas throughout the world. These rules and regulations help local governments ensure that gardens in well-planned residential areas do not become full of unregulated and dangerous constructions. For example, unscrupulous landlords have been known to take advantage of unsuspecting tenants by offering substandard accommodation in sheds.

In the UK, the laws relating to construction of garden buildings are divided into two parts:

- Planning regulations – these cover the size of building that you can build on your property, the use of the building and whether or not you need to apply for permission to build
- Building regulations – these describe the standards to which a building should be constructed.

Overall, the regulations in the UK have a fairly relaxed approach to the construction of dwellings below a certain size and location. However, both planning and building regulations vary between England, Scotland and Wales. Also, different rules apply in national parks and conservation areas. To get the correct details for where you live, you will need to visit your council's planning site for the local rules. The following are some of the general principles to expect.

Planning and proposed use
As a homeowner, you are permitted to build what you like in your garden as long as it fits within certain rules known as

▼ Rules govern where you can build your shed. The position of this US shed wouldn't be accepted in the UK.

'permitted development'. If your shed fits within these rules, you can go ahead and build without any requirement to apply for permission whatsoever. The regulations are set out in detail on the UK government's online Planning Portal (www.planningportal.co.uk) and you should refer to this for the latest information. The guidelines below are the key principles at the time of writing.

SIZE AND HEIGHT
The rules on the size of the building mean that you can cover up to 50% of the area within the curtilage of your property (excluding the area occupied by the dwelling house) with outbuildings. However, this seemingly huge area is then limited slightly by the allowable height and requirements for building regulation approval for buildings over a certain size.

- For buildings within 2m of the boundary, the height is limited to 2.5m
- Further than 2m from a boundary, the maximum height is increased to 3m for buildings with a mono-pitched roof, but with a maximum eaves height of 2.5m
- For buildings with a dual pitched roof, the maximum height is 4m, with a maximum height to eaves of 2.5m
- Sheds are specifically limited to being a single storey.

LOCATION AND USE
In addition to the limits on distance to boundaries mentioned above, the shed should not project forward of the principal elevation of the dwelling house. If you live on a corner plot or have a complex case, you will need to visit the planning website for your area to see how this works for you.

Another aspect of planning concerns the use that is made of the building. Planning rules state that the construction shall be for purposes incidental to the enjoyment of the dwelling house, such as the keeping of poultry, bees, pet animals, birds or other livestock for the domestic needs or personal enjoyment of the occupants of the dwelling house.

This does not include uses such as primary living accommodation.

Garden buildings are often used as offices for the use of the house's occupants, which could be included as a use incidental to the enjoyment of the house. However, if you were to start employing people to work in your garden office, it could then be classed as commercial premises and be subject to a planning application (which could easily be refused) for a change of use.

If you are in any doubt as to whether you are pushing the limits of what is allowed, contact your local council with a sketch showing the location and size of the house and the location, plan size and height of the shed that you are going to build. There will be someone there who can guide you if you need to apply for permission or even what you could do to scale back your design so that it fits within the rules for permitted development.

Before we get too deep into the topic of planning, let's take a quick look at when building regulations apply to garden building construction.

Building regulations

These are a set of design standards that include European and British specifications for materials and dimensions for building work. They normally apply to permanent dwelling houses. Sheds below a certain size are not required to comply with them, but this doesn't mean that you should completely ignore them! What you build needs to be safe and robust for your own safety and peace of mind.

■ If the size is below 15m², building regulations aren't required
■ If your shed is larger than 15m² but less than 30m², is further than 1m from the boundary and is constructed of non-combustible materials, once again, building regulations are not required. (The requirement for a distance from the boundary and non-combustible materials seem to have been introduced as a consideration to protect owners of adjoining properties.)
■ If sleeping accommodation is included in your garden building, you will need to comply with building regulations, whatever the size of your building.

▲ Your shed could become a garden office..

Generally, councils don't have the staff to go around checking on everything that is built in their area. So what happens is that only those buildings that are drawn to the attention of the authorities have action taken against them. These non-compliant buildings are generally reported by neighbours or residents of the area that are adversely affected by the building.

Case study: Andy Clarke (@Workshopshed)

I took an existing shed and enhanced it so I could use it as a workshop. The roof was replaced and insulated. A crumbling plastic wall panel was replaced with tongue-and-groove cladding. An electricity supply was laid from the house. Benches and storage were built into the sides.

I've made furniture, sculptures, tools and models, but I wanted to learn to use metal-working tools and that was not possible in the house because of the noise. The existing shed was draughty and cold but the right size, so with some improvements would work.

Building the internal frame for the double-skinned roof was a challenge as the roof was not actually rectangular, it has a segment cut out of the corner. It took several attempts. There was also a miscalculation of materials, so an extra trip to the wood shop was required.

My advice is that people should get help. It is possible to build a shed on your own but most tasks are a lot easier when there are two of you. Also, if you can't afford insulation then leave some space so you can add it later. And finally, allow for wastage and board sizes when calculating materials.

Shed site safety

Nothing beats the fun of building a shed. However, nothing spoils the fun more quickly than hurting yourself or one of your helpers while doing the job. So here is a quick, but not exhaustive, primer on some of the hazards that you will come across and some suggestions on how to reduce the risk of harm through good planning and using protective equipment.

Let's get started with a couple of definitions. A **hazard** is something that can cause harm during the construction process. This could be the use of sharp tools, working at height or using hazardous chemicals. A **risk** is the chance that one of these hazards will result in harm.

What are the major hazards when building a shed?

- **Cuts and grazes** – You will be working with cutting tools, both hand and electrically powered, that can easily cut/remove fingers
- **Heavy lifting** – Building materials are heavy, and lifting too heavy a weight or lifting in the wrong way can easily cause muscle strain
- **Noise** – Power tools can be noisy, and using them for even relatively short periods of time can damage your hearing

▼ Using a timber base, rather than concrete, can save straining your back.

- **Working at height** – Even though sheds are single-storey buildings, working at any height increases the severity and likelihood of injury
- **Dust** – Traditional hand tools didn't create much dust but power tools do create lots of the stuff.

How to avoid hazards and reduce risks

Once you have identified potential hazards during your project, identify ways that you can remove then reduce them. Or failing that, identify what protective equipment will help reduce the chance of harm.

CONSIDER THE WORK INVOLVED IN CONSTRUCTING A FOUNDATION

Constructing a concrete slab over the whole site on which to build your shed involves a lot of heavy work excavating, transporting materials and then placing concrete. A less strenuous and still acceptable method of building a base is to construct a timber deck on concrete pads (which may also save you money!).

REDUCE TIME SPENT WORKING AT HEIGHT

Working at height is a hazard, so anything that you can do to reduce the time you are constructing the shed roof will reduce the risk of an accident. For the 8 x 6

▲ Construction of a roof at ground level before working at height reduces the risk of falls from height.

project (see pages 72–107), we constructed the roof at ground level to get all the cuts and dimensions right. Working at ground level was easier than climbing a ladder to fit each rafter. Installing the pre-cut timbers on the roof once the walls were in place took much less time, with much less risk.

MAKE SURE YOUR POWER TOOLS ARE SAFE

Reducing the risk from power tools is very much down to making sure that they incorporate the latest safety features. Saws should have the correct guarding and stopping features and for tools that create a lot of dust, there are facilities for dust extraction to remove it at source.

▼ Using a vacuum connected to a power tool removes most dust at source.

PPE: THE LAST LINE OF DEFENCE

The PPE (Personal Protective Equipment) that we used on this project included:

- **Steel toe cap boots** to reduce the chance of damage to feet
- **Protective glasses** to protect the eyes when using the circular and chop saws
- **Gloves** were worn when handling the recycled timber and when doing some of the nailing and fixing.

Noise wasn't a particular issue for this project, but if we had used a belt sander we would definitely have used ear plugs, as well as dust extraction. There was also little finishing work with a sander. If we had done more, we would have also worn dust masks.

▼ Typical PPE you need to have to hand while building your shed.

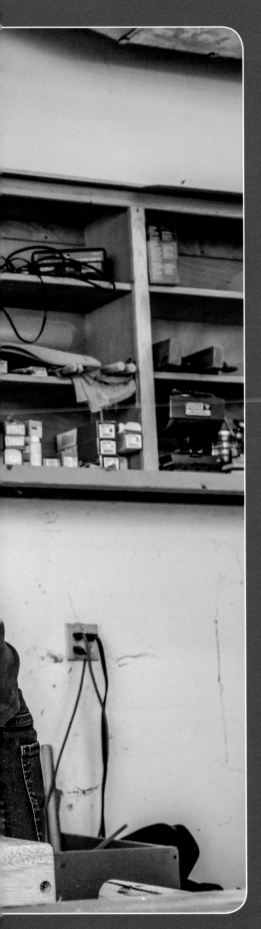

SHED-BUILDING TOOLS & MATERIALS

Whatever tools you have already, a big project such as building a shed is always a good opportunity to buy some more! But you don't need the latest and greatest power tools for a project of this type. You will need to measure accurately and use some basic hand and power tools. We include a description of the tools that we used to build the projects and any specific uses that we found really helpful.

When it comes to building a shed 'You can't make a silk purse out of a sow's ear'. To achieve a quality result you need to start with materials that are going to be up to the task. This doesn't mean that you need to use the finest grades of oak timber for the frame, just that you need to select a timber that will be strong and durable enough for the task. The same applies to other materials, so we give you tips to help you buy durable long-lasting materials.

Measuring tools

There's an old carpenters' saying: 'measure twice, cut once'. Accurately measuring and marking dimensions, angles, levels and straight lines are of key importance to the success of your project.

- **Notebook** – we definitely recommend keeping a paper notebook to hand to record ideas and observations from this and other books. They will help you to pull together your shed design as it develops
- **Plans** – we recommend having a set of plans to build your project. You might create your own or buy a pre-drawn set, which you modify to suit your project. Having a set of plans will help you in many ways, including working out quantities of materials to buy, planning and executing your build
- **SketchUp** modelling software – a free, easy-to-use 3D modelling software used by many woodworkers. Learning to use this software and creating plans and visualisations with it will help to limit your mistakes to the computer screen rather than on site
- **Tape measure** (8m) – longer tapes such as 8m ones are more robust and not as flimsy as smaller measures
- **Pencil/knife** – essential for marking lengths. A carpenter's pencil has a super large lead, which is good for making marks on uneven surfaces and is sharpened

with a penknife. You can use a utility knife to make a line when looking for higher levels of accuracy that are millimetre important
- **Metal ruler** – more robust than the plastic variety and handy for checking and marking smaller dimensions. A metal ruler is best when making marks with a knife, as the blade doesn't catch or mark like it would on plastic or wood
- **Set square** – used for marking and checking that angles are 90 degrees. The limitation of the set square is complemented by the roofing square
- **Roofing square** – enables the marking and measuring of angles
- **Spirit level** – this ensures that the base of the shed is level and the walls are vertical. Don't go for a very short one – a 1m length is about right for this project. Longer ones are available, but can be a bit unwieldy. Short levels don't really average out the variations that occur in the materials that you will be building with for a project of this type
- **Straight edge** – not necessarily a tool, but just a 'trusted' piece of timber that you can use to check things are aligned or for marking out lines on sheet material. It can also be clamped to sheet material as a guide to make sure the circular saw stays on course.

▼ Measuring equipment used to make the sheds in this book.

Hand tools

A tool bucket helps to keep the tools together and stops you wandering around the site looking for a misplaced hammer or screwdriver.

- **Saw** – a basic hand saw is useful for quick cuts and is often quicker than resorting to one of the powered saws described in the next section
- **Hammer** – 'proper' carpenters use perfectly balanced hammers designed for specific jobs. The one they all seem to love is the Estwing brand. No special hammer, though, is required here. A basic robust claw hammer has the ability to remove nails as well as knock them in
- **Mallet** – a wooden mallet is the right weight and a forgiving material for use with the chisel for detailed cutting jobs
- **Chisel** – we used this to cut some of the rebates for the windows, rebates in the door and the hole in the door to accommodate the lock
- **Plane** – for shaping and removing thin slivers of wood. This tool isn't used that frequently in shed building and was only used on one of the projects in this book. It was used on the 8 x 6 Shed (see page 81) for shaping the hip rafters and easing the door, where it fitted rather too snugly in the door frame
- **Clamps** – we used four clamps for the projects in this book: two quick-release clamps with a maximum distance between the jaws of 900mm and two shorter screw clamps. Clamps are essential for holding wood in place while it is cut and shaped. Clamps were used for holding a straight edge in place when cutting sheet materials and 'waney edge' boards
- **Screwdrivers** – although we'd really recommend using a powered drill/ driver for installing most screws, a variety of hand screwdrivers is useful for fitting small numbers of screws, small screws and making adjustments
- **Adjustable spanner** – mainly used for adjusting the base jacks for level and tightening the locknuts. Also used for adjusting and maintaining the chop saw
- **Tin snips** – for cutting the metal trim for the bike shed
- **Scissors** – for cutting the EPDM rubber roof membrane on the Prefabricated Log Cabin (see page 62) and the Bike Shed (see page 123), and the breathable membrane for the 8 x 6 Shed (see page 99).

▲ Having a tool bucket for use on site meant that keeping track of tools was a whole lot easier.

▼ Hand tools used to construct the sheds in this book.

Power tools

It is possible to build all of the structures in this book without power tools. However, they make so many jobs quicker and more accurate that not using them would be a mistake.

You don't need to go for the all-singing, all-dancing, top-quality tools that are used by the pros. Top-quality tools cost more than basic ones and often have features that are only for specific tasks.

At the other end of the market, do you really want to buy a cheap power tool that will have a limited life span? It's a very individual choice and will depend on your level of experience. Do you envisage doing more DIY projects after this one? A cheap tool may last for the duration of the job, but it may also cause you frustration with its lack of accuracy or by going blunt shortly after you bought it.

Some people have a loyalty to a particular brand, especially with the advent of cordless tools, where rechargeable batteries are only interchangeable between tools of the same brand. You can now buy 'bare' power tools that don't have the rechargeable batteries included. The expectation is that the user will already own a pool of batteries suitable for that brand for their other tools.

Here is a short introduction to the tools that I used for this book and my experiences with them:

■ **Drill/driver (drill bits, driver bits)** – I have been using a Bosch corded drill for years. It has been OK, although I have needed a new drill head a couple of times. After building the Prefabricated Log Cabin (see pages 48–71) in the middle of winter I got fed up with managing the electric flex and upgraded to a cordless Makita drill/driver. I wish that I had done it years ago. The freedom of not relying on an electricity supply is liberating. The battery

▲ Mitre saw.

life is excellent and although I have two batteries I never reached the absolute end of the power. I also found that having a combined drill and driver was useful. It was easy to switch between the torque function for tightening screws and the drill function for making holes. Others prefer a dedicated unit for each.

■ **Mitre saw** – I bought this saw several years ago for making furniture. I find it good for cross cutting to length, angles and compound angles. It has been reliable, apart from the turntable cracking on two occasions, but that was quite easy to replace. Most replacement parts are now available for power tools by searching online for the part number along with the brand and model of tool. This DIY maintenance saves on repair costs and extends the life of your tools.

■ **Circular saw** – The circular saw was used for cutting boards and long straight cuts with the grain (ripping). I don't do a great deal of this kind of work and so was lucky enough to be given this tool by an ex-next door neighbour. Thanks Fred Watson.

◀ Corded and rechargeable drills used for this project.

▼ Circular saw.

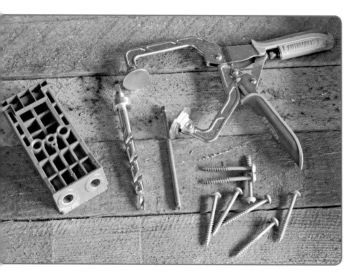

▲ Pocket hole jig (heavy-duty joints).

▲ Pocket hole jig (standard joints).

- **Extension cord (with RCD)** – Working outside or in damp conditions with electrical equipment can be hazardous. Make sure that the supply is sufficiently modern to have an electronic cut-out and the extension cable has a Residual Current Device to detect any damage to the cable before you get any electric shocks.
- **Pocket hole jig** – I bought the Kreg jig for the projects in this book as I was curious to see how well they worked. I enjoyed working with them. Pocket hole joints are a neat and quick way to make joints for smaller shed projects and furniture. The use of pocket hole joints for larger connections such as the frame for the 8 x 6 Shed (see page 76) is less common. The screws are a lot more expensive than standard screws and much, much more than nails. However, the ease of construction, dismantling and adjustability will keep me interested despite the extra cost.
- **Nail gun** – I didn't use a nail gun for any of these projects. I like using a hammer. There was a fair amount of nailing to do for the roof of the Prefabricated Log Cabin (see page 60) and the cabin manufacturer said that it would have saved some time. However, I couldn't justify the purchase of the tool for one project and the time I would have spent going to the hire shop and then returning the tool afterwards didn't seem worth it. If you do a lot of nailing then this tool is worthwhile, but for most DIY projects… not yet.

Green woodworking tools

I introduced a bit of green woodworking (working with unseasoned 'green' timber) to add a bit of additional interest to one of the projects in the book. These tools are quite a specialised little niche and can be found through an online search. To get the skills to use them properly I would recommend that you go on a weekend green woodworking course or find a local green woodworking group.

- **Froe** – This is a forged steel blade. The blade is not sharp, but cuts and splits the log with the force of the mallet
- **Mallet** – This needs to be fairly heavy and is used in combination with the froe for splitting the logs. I made this mallet by cutting away a section of log to form a handle
- **Bike inner tube** – From a bike, can have holes in it. Used to hold a log together while splitting with the froe and mallet
- **Shave horse** – This is a speed clamp that enables you to hold a work piece quickly and easily while shaping it
- **Drawknife** – A sharp blade with two handles that is pulled towards the user to shape the wooden workpiece. Not as dangerous as it sounds….

▼ Green woodworking tools.

Timber

We used a number of different timber species to construct the sheds in this book. There are two main factors influencing the choice of timber for a project: strength and durability.

Strength

A project such as a small shed doesn't tax the strength capacity of timber too much. Timber doesn't necessarily need to have a specific strength grade. Some of the framing timber for the Bike Shed (see page 115) wasn't specifically strength graded. The recycled timber for the 8 x 6 Shed (see page 74) was probably cut and first installed before recent formal grading methods were established. The timbers would, however, have been selected for straightness and lack of imperfection by a roofing carpenter. Although the timbers for the Prefabricated Log Cabin (see page 51) weren't stamped as graded, they came from a reputable supplier of Baltic timber with their own quality control system.

So, although a formal grade of timber isn't required, if you need to buy timber and have a good idea of the strength and consistency that you are buying, then British/European standard BSEN 338 classifies the properties of strength, stiffness and density into different grades. The standard doesn't specify any specific species of timber or appearance, but it guarantees a specific strength, acceptable knots and grain defects. The grading of the timber can be carried out visually by an experienced timber inspector or by passing the lengths of timber through a machine. After the timber has been graded, each piece has

a marking put on it to indicate the grade of timber and other identifying marks.

The reason behind the grading is to simplify the purchasing of timber for the end user. So when you go along to your local timber merchant, the only thing that you really need to know is the grade of timber you need. Even this is relatively straightforward – for most general construction work a grade known as C16 is used.

There are higher grades C24 and lower grades C14, and the price differential between the grades varies from time to time. It can be very little or it can be significant; you will need to check with your timber merchant.

Now that you know a bit about what strength of timber to buy, let's have a look at whether the timber needs any treatment to prolong its life.

Durability

The main factors responsible for timber degrading are persistent damp (which enables fungi to grow and digest the fibres of the wood) and insects (which once again are after the sugar in the cellulose fibres of the wood). If you can keep timber dry and the insects away then timber will last a surprisingly long time. The untreated recycled timber rafters used on the 8 x 6 Shed (see page 74) came from houses built over 60 years ago and to all intents and purposes are as good today as when first installed.

The durability of timber is very much related to the exposure to the elements and whereabouts on a building it is used.

The least exposed elements, Class 1, are above ground framing elements that are within the building envelope. These have little exposure to rain, wind or sun. They get damp occasionally due to condensation from temperature variations and need to be resistant to common insect attack.

Elements that need the most protection, Class 4, are those in contact with the ground. These will be subject to

▼ Typical marking identifying the grade of a piece of timber.

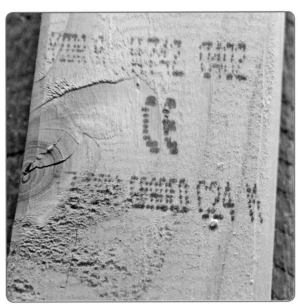

▼ This table from BSEN 335-1 classifies 'exposure' of timber to the elements into four different use classes.

USE CLASS SUMMARY

1	Internal, dry e.g. upper floor joists
2	Internal, risk of wetting e.g. tiling battens
3 COATED	Outdoors, coated, above ground e.g. cladding
3 UNCOATED	Outdoors, uncoated, above ground e.g. fence rails
4	Direct soil or fresh water contact e.g. fence posts

SHED-BUILDING TOOLS & MATERIALS

▲ A sweet chestnut tree provides durable timber.

▼ Table comparing the durability of various timbers in contact with the ground.

Resistance of the ground contact of the heartwood of various woods

Expected duration of ground contact, years	Wood
<5	Alder, birch
10	Spruce, pine
15	Larch
15–25	Oak
>25	Teak

Three standards, EN 350, part 1–2 and EN 460 classifies the natural resistance to rot fungus. EN 350-2 is of particular interest as it presents a classification of the natural durability of the heartwood of a hundred commercially valuable species.

varying persistent dampness, which encourages fungal growth and decay. These need a high degree of protection.

To combat this variation in exposure, building designers can specify types of timber that are particularly durable or have been chemically treated to increase their resistance to decay and insect attack.

The majority of sheds will have a frame made of softwood pine. Although pine is not as durable as other timbers, it is very widely available and when protected from the weather (as for the frame of a shed) needs no further treatment. Much timber in the UK is pressure treated as a matter of course to give it additional resistance to damp and insect damage.

NATURALLY DURABLE TIMBER

Some species of timber are more durable than others. The table opposite gives an idea of the durability of some common timbers that grow in temperate regions. UK-grown species that are very durable include oak and sweet chestnut. Sweet chestnut is very durable and will even resist prolonged contact with the ground.

We used sweet chestnut as external cladding for two projects in this book: for the Bike Shed (see page 116), we used sawn sweet chestnut strips for the vertical cladding and on the 8 x 6 Shed (see pages 86 and 90) we used hand split sweet chestnut shakes on the roof and sawn sweet chestnut planks for the door. It was also used by Ben Law for the frame to the Eco Shed (see page 131) on a third. The big benefits of sweet chestnut are that it is durable, locally grown and also cheaper than oak.

Fixings

Fixings are the collective name given to the bits of metal that hold these sheds together. There is a vast range of nails, screws and bolts on the market. They vary in length, material, diameter and finish – looking through a hardware catalogue it is easy to be overwhelmed by the huge number of specialised fixings for just about any purpose you care to name.

Fixings are made in a variety of materials and with a range of coatings to help them perform their purpose. Standard fixings are made of steel, which itself can have varying properties. Most common fixings have a zinc-plated finish to give a rudimentary resistance to corrosion. This finish is often denoted BZP (bright zinc plated). They are commonly used for internal work.

Galvanising is the most common method of improving corrosion resistance. The thickness of zinc is much greater for galvanised materials, as the item is actually immersed in the liquid metal. Galvanised nails have a rough, dark grey appearance and are used on siding to prevent rust staining.

For higher class and more exposed external work, stainless-steel fixings are used. They are also used when fixing into timbers that are naturally acidic, such as oak and sweet chestnut. The three main categories of fixing are nails, screws and bolts.

Nails

For a given length and diameter, these are the weakest of the fixings. A nail is a simple spike that passes through two pieces of timber, holding them together. The nail is stopped from being pulled out by friction. For most DIY work and small projects, the most common way of fixing nails is still using a hammer.

Screws

With a thread, screws give clamping force, as well as spike. The clamping force is achieved by the screw thread biting into the piece of timber on the point-side of the joint.

Screws come with a wide variety of screw heads:

- **Pozi** – most common
- **Torx** – less common, often used as a security screw
- **Square socket** – used with the Kreg jig
- **Hex** – used on coach screws and longer/stronger screws

Bolts

Bolts are through fixings that clamp the two pieces being fixed together securely.

▼ Tried and tested: hammer and nail.

◄ Types of nails used on the projects in the book. From top left, going clockwise: 75mm long galvanised round wire nails, 50mm long stainless steel annular ring shank nails, 20mm long galvanised felt nails.

Tips

- When fixing sheet material, nail length should be 2.5 times the thickness of the material you are securing
- In hardwood, pre-drill holes to size, no larger than 0.8 diameter.

Tips

- Add PVA glue between the two clamping surfaces for an extra-strong joint
- To prevent splitting of the timber grain, pre-drill the part containing the shank to the same diameter as the screw and the part containing the thread to half the screw's diameter.

◄ Some of the screws used on these projects. From the top left going clockwise: 100mm long coach screws for securing frame members, 63mm long pocket hole screws for pocket hole joints, a variety of stainless steel screws for fixing into sweet chestnut and a variety of multipurpose screws used where corrosion resistance was not critical.

◄ Square neck, dome head coach bolts used for securing wooden blocks for the screw jack feet on the 8 x 6 Shed.

Tips

- Pre-drill hole to maximum diameter of d+2mm
- At least one complete thread to protrude from tightened nut
- Bolts come in different grades, but 4.6 is generally OK for use in wood.

Hardware

There is a vast range of specialised shed hardware to make the construction of your shed easier and more convenient. Two groups of hardware that we focus on here are hinges and locks. However, when developing the design of your shed, consider any fixture or fitting that you would use on your house or any other building as fair game to use in your shed construction.

Also, don't limit yourself to only using metal for the fittings to your shed. You will see the wooden door bolt and roof shakes on the 8 x 6 Shed (see pages 86 and 93). There is a lot of scope for innovation and experimentation on this type of project.

Hinges

This section on hinges focuses on the type of hinges used for board and batten doors. This is the most common type of door used on sheds in the UK. However, as you will see as you read through the projects, most types of hinges can be used for shed doors. Broad butt hinges were used on the Bike Shed (see page 119) and adjustable barrel hinges were used for the Prefabricated Log Cabin (see page 67).

HOW TO CHOOSE SHED DOOR HINGES

The first thing to consider is whether the hinges will be for ornament or security. This section looks at normal utility hinges, but don't give up if you are interested in ornamental hinges. The same principles apply regarding strength and corrosion resistance, although you will be paying more for a more bespoke item.

The majority of utility shed doors are of the 'board and batten' type, which don't have a frame. Hinges for this type of door are of necessity surface mounted. As most shed doors open outwards, the hinges are located on the outside of the shed.

The most common type of shed hinge is the 'T' hinge. This has a short cross to the T for fixing to the door jamb and a long strap that fixes across the face of the door. The major problem with surface-fixed hinges is that the fixings are exposed and accessible to potential intruders.

There are a few ways to make this type of hinge more intruder resistant. The simplest is to use screws with several different types of head. This would include a mixture of traditional slot headed screws, Phillips screws and Torx

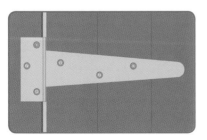

screws. Using this strategy could slow down a thief, but

◀ T hinge fixed with four different types of screw heads.

would not stop an attempt to remove the hinge using a jemmy or crowbar. The crowbar would simply strip the threads out of the wood.

HOW TO MAKE SHED DOOR HINGES MORE SECURE

An improvement on security (and appearance) is to use a dome-headed coach bolt that passes through the hinge and the door ledger. The dome head cannot be turned with a screwdriver. The nut and washer on the back of the door

▶ T hinge fixed with dome-headed coach bolts.

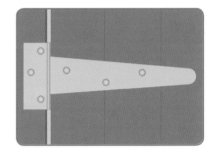

▼ Section showing coach bolts passing through door frame and ledger.

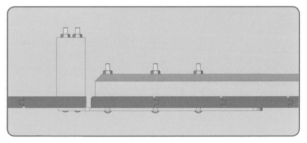

ledger/frame makes it almost impossible to use a crowbar to pull off the door hinge.

Making the door more secure means choosing shed door hinges with thicker metal and larger holes so that you can fit a larger bolt. Typically, an 8mm or 3/8in diameter bolt is OK. From this point, you come up against the law of diminishing returns: it becomes easier for an intruder to break through the door than get an angle grinder to cut the hinge bolts.

What about the strength of the hinge itself?

Shed door hinges come in a variety of lengths and material thicknesses. Generally, a longer hinge made of thicker steel will support a heavier door. And bigger, stronger hinges are more resistant to unwanted attention. The following table gives the strength grading and length from a typical hinge supplier.

An old carpenter's rule of thumb for determining the required length of a T hinge is 'one-third of the width of the door and add one inch for every foot in height'. So, for a shed door that is 2ft 6in wide and 6ft high, a 16in (400mm) long hinge would be needed.

In addition to the hinge material, inspect the hinge pin itself. Is it possible to drive the pin out with the aid of a screwdriver and a few blows of a hammer? If this is the case, it's easier for

◄ Table showing manufacturer's classification of T hinges.

Duty	Length of hinge (mm)
Light	150-200
Medium	300-375
Heavy	400+

an intruder to remove the hinge pins and the whole door than attack the screws securing the hinge to the door.

HOW TO CHOOSE A LONG-LASTING HINGE

When you look in a hardware store, you may find up to four varieties of T hinges made of different materials and with differing finishes. Three of the hinges will be made of mild steel. Mild steel hinges typically come in one of three different protective coatings:

Zinc passivated

These look smoother and shinier than their galvanised equivalent. However, they are only suited to indoor environments. They have less than one-tenth of the protective coating of the galvanised hinge and will most likely start to rust in less than a year outside.

Painted/powder coated (typically black)

The painted or powder-coated hinges rely on the integrity of the coating to protect them from the onset of corrosion. If they are scratched or if the coating is damaged they can be repainted, but the onset of corrosion is difficult to eliminate completely. This finish does look good on antique-effect hinges, so can be used with care.

Galvanised

The king of finishes is galvanising. The item is dipped in a bath of hot zinc to give an irregular/rough, but not unattractive, silvery finish. The coating is 'self-healing' – if the coating is scratched, the zinc corrodes in preference to the steel beneath and forms a coating of zinc oxide that protects the surface beneath.

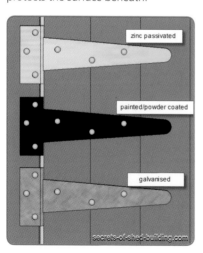

◄ Artist's representation of shed hinge finishes.

The importance of choosing the right coating shouldn't be understated. The cost difference between the zinc passivated and the painted/powder-coated hinges is about

10–15%. The difference between the powder coated and the galvanised is another 10% or so. As you might expect, the more corrosion protection a hinge has, the more it costs – though, in terms of expected lifespan, it is probably worth it. Replacing a hinge that has become covered in rust a couple of years after finishing your shed build is probably not worth the minor cost saving.

You probably won't be interested in the fourth variety of hinge…

The fourth variety of hinge is made of stainless steel. These cost about four times as much as an equivalent galvanised steel hinge. In our view, this type of hinge is not worth the

▲ Stainless steel fittings to a shed hatch.

extra cost for using on your average shed. However, they are highly corrosion resistant. They could be worth considering for a shed that will be exposed to a harsh marine environment for a long time. But, on balance, we think that most beach hut owners manage just fine with galvanised hinges.

Locks

Having considered hinges and security, let's move on to locks and making the lock side of the door as thief-proof as possible.

HOW TO CHOOSE A LOCK

There are four basic lock types you could use: rim locks, pad bolts, hasp and staple, and door bars.

Rim lock

Rim locks are the least secure of the options. The lock is fixed to the inside of the door with wood screws. The door catch secures into a strike plate or keep, fixed to the frame of the door.

Many locks of this type have a latch bolt/spring bolt as well as a deadbolt. This means that the door can be opened and

◄ View of a rim lock set from the outside. Probably the neatest looking of all of the lock types from the outside.

◄ View of a rim lock set from the inside.

closed without locking with the deadbolt. This type of shed door lock is convenient to use and quite unobtrusive as the body of the lock is on the inside of the shed door. But they are also possibly the least secure of the shed door lock options. A determined intruder can easily force the door open as the lock is only held in place by wood screws.

A recent improvement on the traditional rim lock is the 'long throw bolt'-type lock. An excellent example of this is the 'Gatemate'. This product comprises a one-inch square stainless-steel bar that is locked with a high-security six-pin lock.

The stainless-steel bolt has a 'throw' of over two inches, which makes it excellent for use with board and batten doors where tolerances might not be as high as internal environments. The steel 'keep' that the bolt locates into has tolerance, again for doors and structures that move. The metal body of the lock is made of robust steel and comes supplied with security screws.

▼ The 'Gatemate' looks like it is made for the job and it is significantly stronger than other locking systems.

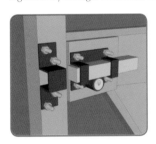
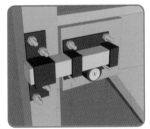

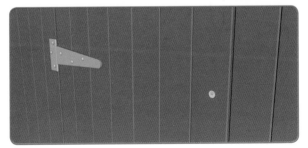

Pad bolt/Brenton bolt

Pad bolts, sometimes called Brenton bolts, are often used to secure garden gates. They consist of a flat or circular bar that slides horizontally within a mounting that is fixed to the outside of the door and door frame. To lock, the bolt is slid horizontally into a receiver that is fixed to the door frame.

The image below is a standard pad bolt. Don't use one of these! They are not lockable. If you choose to use a pad bolt, make sure you get the lockable type, which is the second image below.

Use dome head square neck bolts to secure the housing and receiver to make the fixings as secure as possible. The dome head means that the only way of removing the

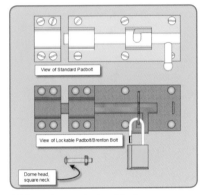

▲ View of a standard pad bolt.

hardware from the outside of the door is by cutting it off. And the bolts pass right through the door frame or the door ledger, so they are held in place very securely.

Pad bolts are available in both zinc passivated, black painted and galvanised finishes. As the bolts will be outside and exposed to the elements, I would recommend using a galvanised finish.

The bolt is locked in place with a padlock. Make sure that you buy an external grade padlock. A padlock that is not built for external use will go rusty and seize up very quickly. Even with an external grade padlock, you will need to oil it once a year to keep the parts moving.

Hasp and staple

The hasp and staple is a similar form of shed door lock to the pad bolt, in that it is fixed to the outside of the shed. The difference is that a hinged hasp is fixed to the door, which when closed goes over a staple fixed to the door frame.

Both pad bolts and hasp and staple fixings are available in a range of qualities. The cheapest are of mild steel, which can be cut with a hacksaw. The higher quality and more expensive branded hardware, such as those made by ABUS, often incorporate parts that are made from hardened steel. Hardened steel has been heat

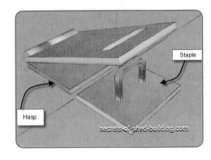

▶ View of the two parts of a hasp and staple.

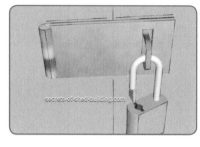
► Closed hasp covers the fixings.

treated, which means that an attempt to cut it with a hacksaw will be much more difficult.

The security of a hasp and staple can be improved by choosing one that has a built-in padlock protector. This is a metal shroud built into the hasp that covers the top section of the padlock. This extra layer of metal makes it more difficult for any would-be thief to cut their way in.

▲ A simple door bar.

Door bars

Door bars are an extra level of security on top of that provided by a lock. The most basic design is a removable steel bar that is locked in place across the mid-height of the door. This bar helps to protect the door lock by preventing the door being moved outwards.

More advanced door bar designs are similar to a huge hasp and staple, with one end of the bar being hinged rather than loose.

For both varieties, the bar fixings should be fixed to the shed frame (rather than the cladding/siding) for maximum security.

Paint and preservatives

The reason for applying additional coatings to the external timber on your shed is to add to the natural durability of the timber and also to alter or enhance the appearance.

If timber is left to age naturally, it will eventually turn a grey colour due to the action of UV light from the sun. On a shed with overhangs and features this won't be uniform and, in our opinion, adds to the natural weathered beauty of the timber.

HOW TO PRESERVE THE NATURAL APPEARANCE OF WOOD

The main thing is not to use varnish! Varnish creates a solid layer that initially is attractive but soon weathers and wherever water manages to penetrate, the coating goes grey and then black. The grey and black are caused by the growth of fungi promoted by the presence of water. The whole building will soon need to be re-varnished, and you will have created a never-ending maintenance task.

The original appearance of the timber can be better achieved by using an oiled finish that incorporates a UV

blocker. This type of finish will be based on the traditional carpenter's boiled linseed oil, but with various additives to screen out the UV and speed up the drying process. This is a bit like sunscreen, and just like sunscreen will require occasional reapplication but it will certainly slow down the weathering of your shed. It can also be used to rejuvenate the appearance of weathered timber.

WHAT IS THE BEST WAY TO CREATE A COLOURED FINISH?

Coloured paint or stains are used to colour a shed to fit in with a garden's colour scheme. Paint and stain sit at two different ends of a spectrum of wood coatings.

Paint is a coating that sits on the surface of the wood and gives a uniform appearance. It is applied to dry timber and it forms an impenetrable skin to protect the timber beneath from UV and water. The problem with paint is that over time the coating loses its flexibility and cracks form in the coating. When water gets through these cracks, it facilitates the growth of fungi. It is also difficult for water to escape through the coating, so the timber can remain damp. If the paint is not scraped back and then recoated on a regular basis, the timber starts to decay and will eventually have to be replaced.

Stain enters the pores of the wood and alters the colour of the wood fibres – it doesn't sit on the surface of the wood. Stain is generally breathable, allowing moisture to pass through and it also contains waxes, encouraging rain from the outside to run off the surface. The benefit of stain is that it is more flexible and, as it is part of the surface, it doesn't allow moisture behind it to initiate decay. Stains do require reapplication at intervals, though the preparation work is less bothersome, often involving just a simple brush down to remove dirt and loose material from the surface. Stains do not give the solid blocks of colour that are achieved with paint and allow the woodgrain below to show through.

Between the two extremes there are semi-transparent stains that contain more solid pigment. As opposed to a pure stain, this sits on the wood surface.

It's a good idea to get a few samples of colour and apply them to the timber you are going to use. This will give you the best idea of how they will look on your project.

▼ Testing different wood finishes for the 8 x 6 Shed.

BUILDING COMPONENTS

Moving on from materials, we now look at some of the systems that are used to enable shed construction. There is a bit of overlap here, as materials of construction such as timber are used for siding. But systems are a combination of the material and fixings and accessories that go with it. For example, EPDM roofing by itself would be good but is made so much better by the adhesive, fixings and trim that are available to create a good-looking, waterproof and long-lasting roof.

Foundations

There is no standard method of creating a shed base. Unfortunately, sheds, sites and performance requirements vary significantly, so you need to have a few different solutions up your sleeve. In this book, each shed has a different type of foundation as they are of such different types.

To give you a head start, here are three of the most commonly used types of shed foundation, roughly in order of ease of construction: pier foundation, timber and stone, and concrete shed base.

Pier foundation

A series of pads to support the timber foundation beams provide support, while requiring fewer materials than a full-blown concrete slab. These foundations are equally useful for large and small sheds; it is only the size and spacing of the pad foundations that will vary. Foundations such as these are extremely useful if you need to build on a sloping site.

Each of the individual piers can be built to a common top level. A grillage of timber beams supported on screw jacks provides the final fine-level adjustment. Also, if the need arises to move your shed, then the foundations can be taken up much more easily than a full concrete slab.

▼ Shed pier foundation enabling a shed to be built on a steep slope.

ADVANTAGES OF PIER FOUNDATIONS

■ Cheaper than laying a concrete slab, as a lot less concrete is required
■ Simple to build, so a specialist contractor is not necessary
■ Environmental benefits, in so much as less concrete is needed and you will not be adding any foreign materials to the soil on which you are building
■ Very little excavation to begin building
■ Very little spoil to dispose of from the build site
■ Can save you a good deal of time, as you can immediately begin to build once you have your materials gathered
■ Can increase longevity of your shed by lifting the shed floor off the ground so that moisture from the ground cannot rise and damage the timber structure.

In short, using a shed pier foundation can save you both time and money.

INSTALLING PIER FOUNDATIONS

You must first do a bit of excavation to level up the ground at the location of each pier. The exact location of the piers is dependent on the size and layout of the floor beams.

The depth of the piers will depend on the size and use of

▲ Shed floor under construction. Piers in this case are made of cast concrete rather than stacked concrete blocks.

▲ Shed foundation excavation.

the shed and also the ground conditions. You will not need to dig a hole as deep as a house foundation as sheds are tolerant of some ground movement. But you will need to remove the topsoil and get down to a level of soil that is solid enough; soil in which you find it difficult to leave a heel mark from your boot.

Concrete blocks

The simplest form of pier foundation uses standard concrete building blocks. The concrete blocks are laid one on top of another and bonded together with mortar so that they cannot shift. To get the tops of the blocks level, shims made up of sections of paving slab or pressure-treated timber can be used for the finer adjustment. The timber floor joists are then supported on this grid of concrete blocks.

Timber and stone

A storage shed foundation for small- and medium-sized sheds on level ground can be built quickly and cheaply using crushed stone and pressure-treated timber bearers.

BUILDING A SHED BASE BEGINS WITH THE SETTING OUT

Start by marking out the corners of the shed. It is best to use timber pegs made from 2 x 2in (50 x 50mm) timber, sharpened at one end. Knock a nail into the centre of each peg and set up a string line around the perimeter. Check the rectangular shape that you have marked out by measuring across the diagonal. If the dimensions across each diagonal are equal then the corners are true squares.

There are many ways of controlling the level of an excavation, using sighting rails and optical levels. However, for a small excavation like this it is best to keep it simple – a spirit level used together with a long (8ft or 2.4m) 4 x 2 timber will be fine.

Using a spade, do an initial strip of the turf and topsoil to a depth of 50mm (you can use the soil for landscaping elsewhere in the garden).

Excavate to the finished depth of 75mm in one corner and then, resting the end of the long 4 x 2 on this corner peg, measure down to ground level. Cut a piece of timber to

this measured length. Continue the excavation, checking at intervals that you are not going too deep using the 4 x 2, spirit level and measured length of timber.

SELECTING CRUSHED STONE FOR A SHED BASE

The stone to be used for constructing the storage shed foundations should be what is known as 'well graded material'. This means that there is a good mix of stone sizes from about 40mm diameter down to very fine dust. The best material for this in the UK is sold as Department of Transport Type 1. However, for the purposes of constructing a shed, crushed stone or pulverised concrete should be adequate. Just make sure that you don't use gravel or a single-sized aggregate for a shed base, as this will not compact or lock together.

This sketch shows a detail through the edge of the storage shed foundation. The underside of the timber should be above the general ground level. Lawn edging has been included to give the shed foundation a neat appearance and make it easier to cut the grass.

▼ Edge detail showing separation of stone, earth and grass.

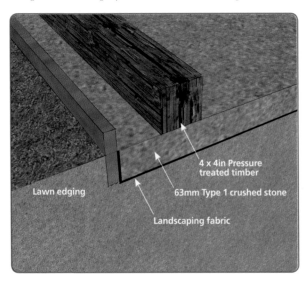

Lawn edging

4 x 4in Pressure treated timber

63mm Type 1 crushed stone

Landscaping fabric

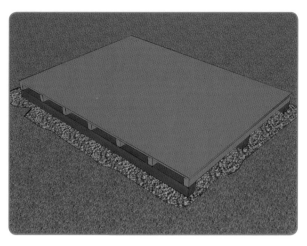

▲ Shed base with deck.

Use landscaping fabric here for two reasons:

1   To keep the stone separate from the soil. Over time, without a separation layer, the stone can sink into the ground and the foundation will soften (particularly on clay ground).
2   Weeds and vegetation will have a hard time growing beneath the shed due to a lack of light, but as the stone can extend about 6in beyond the shed wall, the fabric helps to keep the weeds down.

The landscaping fabric should be a heavy-duty material, which is permeable to water.

PLACING THE CRUSHED STONE LAYER

Before compacting the stone, rake it as level as possible. You could hire a vibrating plate, but if you need a bit of exercise use a hand tamper to compact the ground. Hand tampers comprise a 10kg weight with an area of approximately 4 x 4in (100 x 100mm), which you raise and drop repeatedly to compact the stone. Pound the stone down until it's compacted and even, remembering to keep checking the levels in the same way that you did for the excavation. Add or remove material where necessary to achieve a level platform.

LAYING THE PRESSURE-TREATED WOOD FOUNDATIONS

Check that you lay these timbers perpendicular to the direction of the floor joists in the shed floor. The pressure-treated timbers should be 4 x 4in (100 x 100mm) to allow ventilation beneath the shed. Pressure-treated timber already has a long life when in contact with the ground, but installing the weed barrier and stone should prolong its life further. Moisture is the element that starts decay, so anything you do to keep the timbers dry is time well spent.

The spacing of the timber bearers should be in the instructions for the shed kit you are building or in the shed plans if you are building a shed from scratch.

▼ Layout of base support timbers.

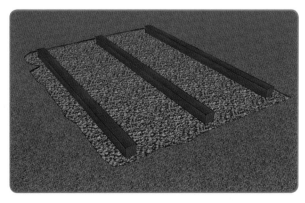

One tip to prolong the life of your shed floor is to install and nail down a strip of polythene or bitumen damp-proof membrane (DPM) along the top of each base timber. This will stop moisture getting into your shed floor from contact with the timber foundation beams. The timber below the DPM will still remain relatively dry, as it is above the general ground level and beneath the shed.

Before the storage shed foundation can be considered complete, do a final check for level along the length of each timber and between timbers.

Concrete shed base

A concrete shed base can also double as a concrete shed floor.

A floating concrete foundation is typically 75–100mm (3–4in) thick, which, despite moving slightly, should last as long if not longer than the shed built on top. The slab can be plain (unreinforced) concrete or a light mesh of steel reinforcement can be added for extra strength and to control cracking.

ADVANTAGES OF A CONCRETE SHED BASE

Although this type of foundation is more expensive than the types already described, a concrete shed floor does have advantages:

■ There is no need to build a separate shed floor
■ It can be hosed down if it gets dirty or wet
■ The floor can be built closer to ground level, thus minimising the need for steps or a ramp
■ A concrete shed base is very durable, so damp garden machinery can be left there and there is no danger of the floor rotting as a timber floor could.

A disadvantage of having a concrete floor is that it can be cold on the feet if you are using the shed as a workshop or hobby room. If you intend to use a shed with a concrete floor for these purposes then a timber sub-floor or an insulated screed will make the floor a lot warmer.

HOW TO BUILD A CONCRETE SHED BASE

The main items of work are:

1. Excavation
2. Formwork
3. Mixing concrete
4. Placing and finishing the concrete.

1. Excavation

If the area of your shed is firm and dry then remove the topsoil to a depth of 100mm. Place a layer of stone to a depth of 50mm. If the ground is not so good you may wish to increase the depth of stone or in local areas to get rid of 'soft' spots.

2. Formwork

The perimeter formwork for a concrete shed base will most likely be 18mm (¾in) plywood with 50 x 50mm timber stakes knocked into the ground at 600mm (2ft) centres. The formwork should be set up off the level stone/earth base, so that the top is level all the way around and that none of the posts stick up above the top of the formwork. The formwork needs to be sufficiently robust that it will be able to contain the wet concrete and act as a guide for the timber straight edge tamper when it comes to levelling the concrete surface. The area of the pour should be lined with a polythene damp-proof membrane (DPM). The purpose of this membrane is twofold:

1. To stop loss of water from the wet concrete into the ground during pouring (this would weaken the concrete).
2. To keep the contents of the shed drier by creating a barrier to water from the ground penetrating up through the slab.

The specification for the polythene DPM will be 1200 gauge; the brand name 'Visqueen' is commonly used in the UK. If laps are needed in the membrane, these should be a minimum of 350mm and sealed with a suitable tape obtained from a builders' merchant.

3. Mixing concrete

The main methods of obtaining concrete are by mixing your own or buying in a ready-mixed supply. If you are mixing your own concrete, hire a concrete mixer for the day, as it will make this heavy work a lot easier. Each cubic metre of concrete weighs about 2.5 tonnes. A 4in thick 10 x 12ft

shed base will have over a cubic metre of concrete in it, so be prepared for some work here!

Concrete is a mixture of cement, sand (fine aggregate) and coarse aggregate. Mixes vary in their proportions depending upon the properties required. For concrete for a shed base, order 'ballast' from your builders' merchant. This is a mixture of fine and coarse aggregate. Mix the ballast with cement in the ratios recommended by the supplier – 1:5 (cement:ballast) by volume is typical. Add water to the mix in small amounts, keeping the mix on the dry side (a sloppy mix will be hard to handle and will result in poor-quality concrete).

Alternatively, contact your local ready-mix supplier and order a suitable truck mix. Ready-mix concrete suppliers have a range of concrete mixes – for a shed base, specify a minimum of C20. This means that it will be designed to have a crushing strength of at least 20N/mm² after 28 days. Be prepared for a bit of work transporting the wet concrete to the site and consider what ramps you may need to get the wheelbarrow up steps or over other obstacles.

4. Placing and finishing the concrete

Place the concrete from the barrow starting at one corner and working outwards. The concrete should be placed evenly and slightly proud of the formwork. The concrete is finished using a timber straight edge (4 x 2in). Starting at one end of the slab, level the concrete off, moving the edge side to side as you progress. With the concrete shed base levelled off you now have a 'rough tamped' finish.

When the slab is complete, cover it with polythene or damp hessian sacking. The purpose of the covering is to keep the moisture in. Concrete does not dry, it 'cures' – if the surface becomes dry during the first three days it will become dusty and weak.

Concrete gains strength slowly. The longer you keep the covers on the better. The concrete will be stiff the next day, but the surface will mark if you walk on it. Concrete gains its design strength after 28 days (this is a standard strength test on commercial concrete pours). However, after seven days it will be fine for the next stage of construction.

With the concrete shed base finished, you are now ready to start building the rest of your shed.

▼ Detail of completed concrete foundation.

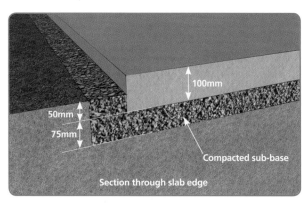

100mm

50mm

75mm

Compacted sub-base

Section through slab edge

▼ Section through edge of formwork.

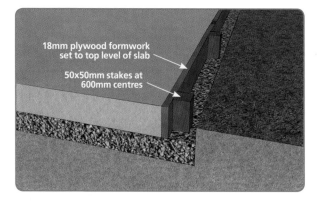

18mm plywood formwork set to top level of slab

50x50mm stakes at 600mm centres

Roofing

The most common types of shed roof design are pent, gable and hipped roofs. In addition, there are other less common roof types that you might want to consider. Before you decide which you are going to build, it's worth reviewing each of the types below and seeing how they are framed. You can then decide which is best for your project, based on a mixture of appearance and your own skills and expertise.

Popular types of shed roof design

PENT

This design has the simplest form. Its single slope is suited to buildings that sit against a fence or wall. The roof is a simple beam spanning between the front and back walls. The roof pitch is governed by the choice of roof-covering materials and any planning restraints. The span of the roof is limited by the strength of the timber roof joists – for longer spans, a mono-pitch truss could be used.

Advantages of a pent roof
- Good for areas where shed height is limited
- Porch/shade structure can be made from overhang
- Low roof pitch means that roof covering must be sheeting, felt or Ethylene Propylene Diene Monomer (EPDM) membrane, a synthetic rubber used in a range of applications.

GABLE

The roof of a gable shed is a simple duo-pitch roof truss. Storage can be achieved in the roof, or headroom can be increased by raising the bottom chord of the truss to form a raised collar truss. The angle of the shed roof can vary widely from a typical 20 degrees on mass-produced sheds to 70 degrees on a high-pitched gable roof shed. (When a roof slope exceeds 70 degrees the British Standard defines it as a wall!)

▲ Pent roof allotment shed.

▼ Framing arrangement of pent roof shed.

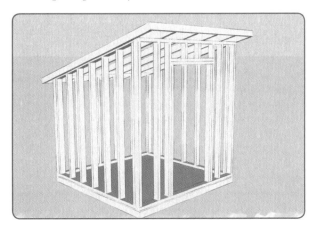

▼ Framing arrangement of gable shed, with room for storage in the roof.

▼ A nice-looking gable-roofed shed.

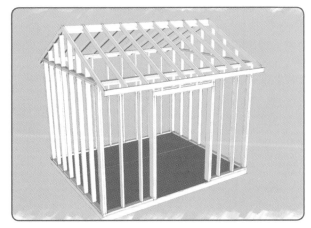

▲ Hip roof shed with timber shake roof.

▲ Group of curved roof sheds.

Advantages of a gable roof
- Suits all types of shed roof covering
- Loft/storage space can be incorporated in the roof, but less than with a gambrel roof (see below).

HIP
Sheds with hip roofs are similar to gable roof sheds, but the end wall slopes in so that all four faces of the roof slope towards the ridge.

Hip roof-framed sheds are less common than gable roof sheds, as the framing is more complex due to the compound mitres where the jack rafters meet the hip rafters.

The hip roof shed has a visual advantage in that the sloping ends reduce the bulk of the roof, thus improving its appearance. The sloping ends do, however, reduce the potential for storing stuff in the roof. This style of shed roof is commonly used for pool house sheds and summerhouses where roof storage is rarely an important criteria.

Less common types of shed roof design
SALT BOX
This originated as a fisherman's shed, and was designed for its simplicity and strength to resist the wind coming in from

the sea. This shed roof design is not symmetrical; one of the eaves is a lot lower than the other. The design is an extension of the gable roof with one side of the roof forming a 'lean-to' extension or 'cat-slide' roof.

CURVED
Curved roofs do have a certain visual appeal. There are not too many immediately apparent structural or other advantages, but they are worth considering for their visual novelty.

GAMBREL
This achieved prominence in Dutch Colonial architecture. Structures with gambrel barn roofs allowed animals and equipment to be stored downstairs with a hayloft upstairs.

The smaller modern form of this type of shed (for garden use, not farms) is popular in the US but less common in the UK, probably due to planning height restrictions.

Advantages of a gambrel roof
- Traditional and popular shape in some parts of the world
- Large volume of space for storage can be incorporated in the roof.

▼ Salt box-style shed under construction.

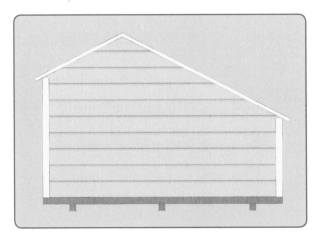

▼ Profile of gambrel-style shed.

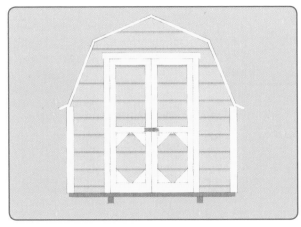

Roof pitch

The primary purpose of a shed roof is to protect you and your possessions from the weather. To make a roof waterproof, the roof pitch/slope will influence the materials you choose. Roofs can be classified into three broad groups according to roof slope:

FLAT ROOFS: PITCH = 0–10 DEGREES

Roofs with a pitch below 10 degrees are known as 'flat roofs'. For a shed with this roof slope, EPDM, bitumen mineral felt on plywood decking, or sheet metal will be the main options.

Flat roofs have experienced problems over the years with leakage and durability. The main reason is that water is not sufficiently 'encouraged' to drain off the roof. Whatever you do, don't use a 'dead flat' roof (pitch = 0 degrees). Make the roof slope at least six degrees to ensure some positive drainage. Also, if the roof is insulated, you should include a ventilated air gap between the insulation and roof deck to stop condensation.

LOW PITCH ROOFS: PITCH = 10–20 DEGREES

Tiles or shingles may be used for roofs with these slopes with caution. Extra care must be taken with waterproof underlay and following the manufacturer's recommendations.

PITCHED ROOFS: PITCH = 20 DEGREES+

Concrete interlocking tiles are really the only tile suitable at a 20-degree pitch. They are rarely used on small timber structures due to their heavy weight, large size and unattractive appearance. Clay tiles, in contrast, particularly handmade ones, make for a roof with a lot of character. However, clay tiles need a minimum pitch of about 35 degrees.

Roof coverings

As if there weren't enough decisions to be made with roof style and slope, you also need to choose a roof covering that you are happy with. Choice of roof materials should be a decision made on appearance, durability and cost.

Appearance

Beauty is definitely in the eye of the beholder, but the most appealing sheds often use roofing shingles. Wooden shingles or clay tiles are really 'where it is at' in respect of craftsman-style roofs and you will see these in two of the sheds in this book. A modern and increasingly popular alternative is the green or living roof. Green roofs utilise low-maintenance plants that grow in a substrate on top of the waterproof membrane.

Durability and cost

For these two factors, clay tiles and shingles are at the top end of the pricing range. But when it comes to durability, there is a real stand-out performer when you look at the total cost per year. And it isn't mineral roof felt that is the current 'go to' choice of British shed owners. This has a typical life of five years or so and a cost per year of double our recommended option which is…

EPDM rubber. This material has been around in industrial environments for roughly 50 years. It has a good, tried and tested pedigree and is increasingly being used on domestic houses and sheds. It has an expected life in excess of 40 years and is used as roofing on two of the sheds in this book.

Cost summary

The table below summarises the cost per square metre and lifespan of each material, divided to give a cost per year, which is a good way to compare the whole life cost of these materials.

EPDM RUBBER

EPDM rubber is a sheet membrane that is delivered in a single

▼ Comparison of whole life costs for roofing materials.

Roofing Type	Expected life (yrs)	Initial cost (£/m²)	Cost/yr/m²
EPDM	40	10	£ 0.25
Mineral roof felt (polyester fibre)	10	5	£ 0.50
Mineral roof felt	5	3	£ 0.60
Fibreglass	25	15	£ 0.60
Felt tiles/Roofing shingles	15	10	£ 0.67
Clay tiles	50	40	£ 0.80
Onduline	15	15	£ 1.00
Cedar shingles	30	35	£ 1.17

▲ EPDM roof with raised seams to mimic a lead roof.

sheet to fit the size of roof where it is to be installed. It has been used on commercial and factory building roofs for over 40 years. It is now being promoted more extensively for sheds. It is especially suited to flat roofs, but can be used on roofs of any pitch. EPDM is also especially suited to green roofs.

GREEN ROOFS

Green roofs are beautiful. They utilise a waterproof membrane on the roof deck with a build-up of growing medium on top. Modern green roofs use a relatively thin layer of growing medium that particularly suits hardy succulent plants.

MINERAL ROOF FELT

The standard garden shed will come with a roof covered in cheap mineral roofing felt. This system does the job of keeping the water out, but is fragile and relatively short-

▲ Green roof with a variety of succulent plants.

▼ Shed with newly installed cedar shingle roof.

▲ Coloured felt roofing shingles.

◄ Shed with standard roofing felt.

▼ Shed with clay roof tiles.

lived. A bit of unseen damage to the shed roof covering will allow water in and cause damage to the structure of the shed.

Standard shed felt is formed of bitumen-impregnated fibres and lasts about five years. An improved version of the shed felt with a base of polyester fibres impregnated with bitumen is more durable and lasts for approximately 15 years.

The cheaper felt is often supplied as standard on pre-made sheds to keep the 'sticker' price down, with the longer-lasting felt available as an upgrade.

FIBREGLASS

Fibreglass is not commonly used as a shed roofing material, though we have seen it on a fisherman's hut on a Dorset beach, probably for extreme durability. The fibreglass shell would resist the winter storms and sand blasting around the beach, as well as be extremely secure. Not sure it is a thing of beauty, but it should last well.

FELT TILES OR ROOFING SHINGLES

Using felt tiles is the next step up in quality. Roofing shingles are laid starting at the bottom of the roof. The shingles overlap each other by about 150mm and at the ridge a capping piece is used. This roof finish is a vast improvement on using a roll of mineral felt and is much more durable.

▲ Onduline roof.

▶ Metal shed roof with edge flashing.

CLAY TILES

Clay tiles are available in a huge range of colours, sizes and shapes and give the building a sense of place and permanence. Typically, the best choice is to match the style of the roof to your house or other buildings in the area.

A note of caution on using clay tiles for shed roofing: they are heavy! The supporting roof and walls must be made strong enough to support them.

ONDULINE – CORRUGATED BITUMEN SHEET

Corrugated bitumen-impregnated fibre makes for a durable roofing system. Most likely suited to slightly larger sheds, it is durable and quite cheap.

WOODEN SHINGLES

Cedar roofing shingles can make a roof look special. The basic installation process is to fix them to battens with a layer of underlay beneath.

SHEET METAL

Corrugated metal is widely used on larger commercial sheds and buildings. It can look complex and hard to work with for the DIY builder, but this need not be the case. It can be an economical and very durable option if you take some time to investigate how the various metal roofing systems work, what tools to use and the best places to buy the materials and fixings.

▼ Beach hut with fibreglass roof for high durability.

Walls

Most shed walls in the UK are constructed with a timber cladding. Timber is good at keeping out the weather, is relatively long lasting with some maintenance, and it is also reasonable at keeping out intruders. It does all of this at a reasonable price. Other material options include polythene, fibre cement, steel and aluminium. These all have their own properties and 'wrinkles'.

All of the projects in the book have timber on the outside of one type or another. The most basic is a single skin wall but it is easy to build in the possibility of adding insulation at a later date with a bit of forward planning.

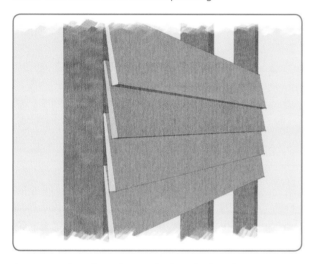

▲ **1** Section through overlapping feather edge boarding.

▼ **2** Section through overlapping shiplap boarding.

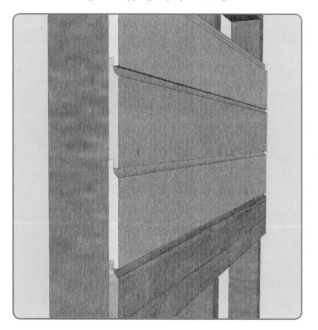

Types of wood cladding

The sketches below show the different types of wood cladding:

1 The most basic is made of overlapping timber boards, fish-scale style, to shed the water. This type of cladding was used on the 8 x 6 Shed (see page 95).

2 This is what is known as shiplap boarding with the edges machined to overlap and give a flush face.

3 This picture shows match boarding where the boards actually interlock, one into the next.

Of these three styles of wooden cladding, the match boarding is the most weathertight as any distortion within a board is restrained by the connection to the board above/below. With the other two styles, a gap opens up if the board warps, which creates a draught when the wind blows or a leak when it rains and the wind blows!

The Prefabricated Log Cabin (see page 57) used a 'very beefy' version of match boarding. For that shed the cladding also formed the wall structure without the need for an internal frame.

Multi-layer walls for higher performance

For a shed that requires extra protection from the elements, such as a garden office or outdoor recreation room, a different sort of wall is more appropriate. This type of wall is made up of an outer skin known as a 'rain screen cladding' or simply 'siding' and serves to form a physical barrier to

▼ **3** Section through overlapping interlocking match boarding.

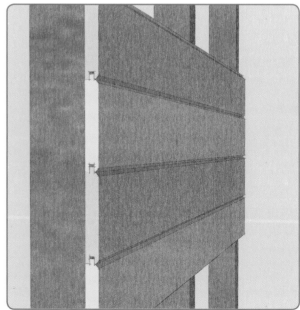

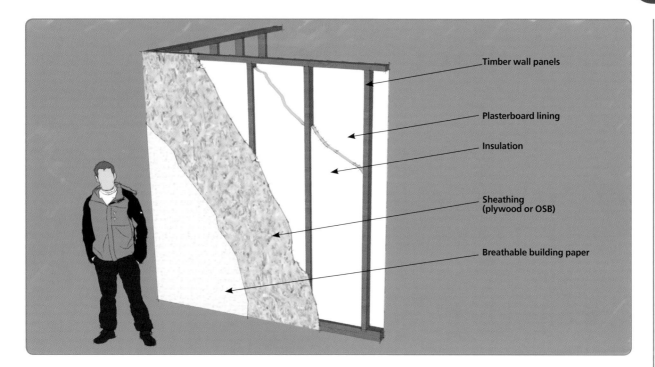

Timber wall panels

Plasterboard lining

Insulation

Sheathing
(plywood or OSB)

Breathable building paper

protect the layers behind – weatherboard, shiplap and match boards are perfect for this, along with other types of metal, PVC and cement sheet cladding. If some rain penetrates the external screen then it is stopped by the breathable building paper, which is fixed to the structure beneath. This layer also stops draughts getting in through panel joints.

An internal structural skin is nailed directly to the vertical timber studs that make up the shed's framework (and carry the roof loads), which is known as 'sheathing'. This sheathing helps to brace the overall structure against horizontal loads. This type of wall separates the structural and shielding functions of the wall.

Insulated shed walls are useful for sheds or buildings that are being used as garden offices or outdoor garden rooms. They allow you to comfortably enjoy the peace of your room without exposure to extremes of heat or cold. Non-insulated walls are good for sheds that are being used for storage, holding overflow from your house, camping equipment, storing Christmas decorations, or anything else you may have to find a space for.

The Eco Shed in this book was built with a multi-layered wall approach. This had the function of minimising draughts in such a large space and also giving the option of adding insulation at a later date if needed.

Case study: Dan Keeley

I built a fairly traditional wooden-framed shed with shiplap cladding. It is L-shaped, with the smaller part being a traditional shed-type affair. I built it primarily as an office because I was approaching a significant working from home stint – and at the time we had very young children – so working in the house was not an option due to the noise!

The main office area is about 5 x 3m and has no internal supports, so is a nice big open space (it also serves as a brewing space, as well as office!). It has a full professionally installed/signed off electric system, and is generally as comfortable as being in the house, but with a better view!

I've built a plethora of playhouses, treehouses, chicken runs, etc, and also put together the greenhouse. We also fitted our kitchen, which involved removing a wall too.

The trickiest thing was probably the roof – thankfully I had help with that from a builder neighbour, and his roofer friend. The hardest bit was calculating the angles for the roof struts – once done and proven right we were able to just copy a template piece. Storms removed the professionally fitted felt from the roof – thankfully another roll of felt and a LOT of nails seems to have repaired it. So far.

My best tip is to get the windows FIRST, THEN design the shed! All my windows apart from one were free, unwanted from upgrades. The large window at the back is actually brand new, and top spec glass, but as it was a cancelled order, I got it for £40, which is a bargain! Also, the more window you have, the less the cost of cladding. I also recommend underfloor heating – this works really well, especially when combined with wall and roof insulation (just the electric mat stuff).

Windows

Shed windows can be one of the most influential design elements of the shed, second only to the style of the roof. Sometimes it seems that when people set out to build their shed they pay a good bit of detail to everything except the windows, so the shed windows get the short end of the stick. This can be very unfortunate indeed when you consider the fact that the windows can influence the look, feel and style of the shed.

The two sheds below are a good example, very similar apart from the windows. The shed on the left with the small windows and double doors would be a good storage shed, whereas the shed on the right with the larger opening windows, to give better control of ventilation and let in more light, would function better as a workshop.

Frame materials

One of the first choices you will have to make concerning your windows will be to decide what sort of material you will need for your window frames. The three main material choices for the window frame construction are wood, PVC and aluminium. Each has its own individual characteristics:

- **Wooden window frames** look beautiful when properly treated or painted. If they are neglected, they will become weather damaged in the longer term
- **PVC window frames** usually come in predetermined colours and do not lose their paint over time as the material itself is dyed. The problem with PVC is that over time it can become brittle, fade and is not so environmentally friendly at the end of its life
- **Aluminium** is long-lasting and does not rust easily. Aluminium windows are durable and can come in a

variety of anodised finishes that give good corrosion resistance with little maintenance. Aluminium can be expensive, but this is your shed you are building here, so it could be worth it.

Glass

Your next choice is the type of glass you will need to use in your windows. Much of this choice will be based on the intended use for your shed. If you will be using your shed for plain storage, you might consider **plastic or standard glass window panes**.

If you will be growing plants then you might want to consider using a **horticultural glass**, which is thinner and lets more heat pass through. It is fragile though, and breaks into sharp shards when broken.

If you want a window that will both look good and be much more energy efficient then a **double-glazed window using toughened glass** is going to be your best option.

Window styles

Now you must decide which style of window you prefer or need.

If all you are looking for is a source of light, to be able to see out, and ventilation is not too much of a concern, then a **fixed window** may be exactly what you need.

For a simple window that looks nice but is more functional than beautiful then you might consider either a **side hung** or **top hung casement**.

If you are looking for a beautiful window for your garden office shed then you might choose to install **double hung sliding sash windows** or **horizontal sliding sash windows**.

▼ Choosing different windows and finishing trims can significantly change the appearance of your shed.

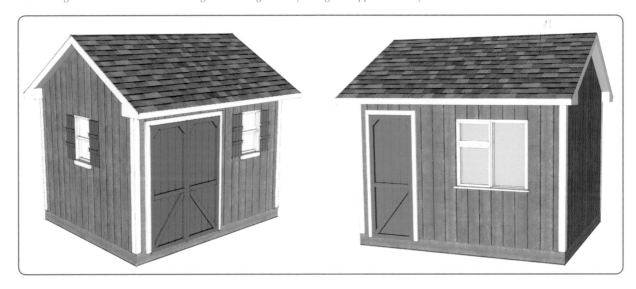

◆ Varying styles of shed window.

Storage shed windows come in a wide range of shapes and styles. These different styles can make a world of difference in the look and overall feel of your shed.

SECURITY WINDOWS

Security windows are horizontal, very narrow, non-opening and usually set very high on the walls of the shed. This style of window lets in light but is above most people's eye level (so preventing the casual passer-by from determining the contents of the shed) and is too narrow a slot for anything to be lifted in or out.

If you are not looking for quite this level of security then smaller windows set at the standard height can improve security. Also, steel bars set vertically into the frames on the inside of the glass will do the trick without being too intrusive.

SHUTTERS

One last thing that you might consider is to install shutters or blinds. Shutters can provide security when they are functional due to the fact that they can be closed and locked. They can also provide shade from the sun. Blinds serve a similar purpose. They protect from the sun and provide security by obscuring the contents of the shed from outside viewing.

Where to buy shed windows

Your shed windows can be obtained from various sources, most commonly new ones from a home supply store and used ones. If you are looking to save a bit of money then the second option would be a good choice. Used windows can be picked up from properties that may be getting refurbished, or bought from businesses that specialise in reclamation of used building materials.

◆ Shed window with shutters.

SHED 1: PREFABRICATED LOG CABIN

1. Assessing the site

This project is for a shed to be used by a family to improve and maintain their general fitness. We checked that there was space in the garden to build a shed that could house a treadmill, an exercise bike, some free weights and a punch bag.

Potential sites

The two potential sites were:

1 At the front of the house where the garden had been used as a children's play area
2 At the rear of the back garden, against a fence.

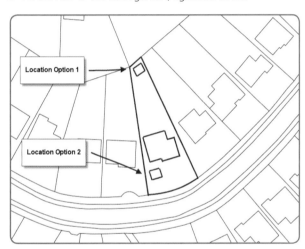

The problem with the first area was that, under permitted development rules, a planning application is required for any development forward of the front elevation of the house. This would have cost money and taken time, and there was no guarantee that the application would have been granted.

The problem with the second area was that there was already a shed in the chosen spot (though slightly dilapidated) and an overgrown hedge where the bushes had become small trees. The rear boundary fence was also in bad repair.

We went for option two. It involved a little bit of site preparation work, but this needed to be done anyway. One benefit of doing this was that we discovered that the garden was bigger than we had thought and so the new gym wouldn't project quite so far into the garden as initially planned.

◀ Image plan of site.

▼ Site where shed is to be built.

Construction and style decisions

The next step was to decide on the construction method and style of shed. The client was keen to get the gym operational as soon as possible, so the shed was to be built in December when the weather isn't great and days are short.

A number of neighbours had built cabins of the popular Scandinavian interlocking log style. The feedback was that these had been successful and worked well in the local climate. Bearing this in mind, we went for a prefabricated cabin kit. That was the straightforward part!

The delivery period after placing the order was four weeks. This gave us time to clear the site, dispose of debris and then construct a base ready to support the cabin kit when it arrived.

From among the myriad options, we looked closely at the following:

- Wall thickness
- Shed base
- Roof covering
- Glazing
- Insulation.

▲ Image of cabin on instructions, including mud, coffee and rain.

WALL THICKNESS

We chose a 45mm wall thickness as a good compromise for the size of cabin and use. Thinner logs might not have sufficient thickness to resist the weather; thicker logs were more suited to residential-type use.

SHED BASE

The supplier offered an adjustable plastic base as an extra to the system. We opted for a more beefy steel jack system with a timber grid on top to support the walls of the cabin and the timber floor bearers. This also had the advantage of lifting the whole cabin out of contact with the ground and allowing air to flow underneath. Damp is the main cause of timber decay and so taking steps to eliminate this prolongs the life of the shed.

ROOF COVERING

Bitumen felt roofs have a limited life. After a period they slowly lose their ability to keep water out. This isn't a sudden thing. The first time that most people realise this is when they suddenly have a wet cabin and a large section of roof needs replacing. In Chapter 3 we looked at the advantages of EPDM (Ethylene Propylene Diene Monomer), which is a type of synthetic rubber and should outlast the shed (and many shed owners).

Case study: Dwayne Goode

My shed is timber framed with steel cladding and it has polystyrene insulation in between the timbers with plasterboard on the inner walls. I managed to pick up 2 x 3 metre windows and designed it around those.

I have always wanted a decent-sized shed and money was always an obstacle, but when my mate Ali asked me to help him build his, I decided it was well past time for me to get one built. I am fortunate that I have a rather large garden but hate gardening and my wife isn't keen either, so she told me to build what I wanted. I checked the Planning Portal for the council and found the biggest I was allowed without going through the hassle of planning permission and went with that. I have various machines in there including a Harrison 14in lathe, home-made milling machine, 3-D printer, a part-built CNC router/laser and various other tools.

Getting started was the hardest bit, but in the actual build itself I would say getting the concrete base sorted was the most exhausting part, as it was all done by hand. I did have a mixer though. I didn't have any major mishaps. I did have an incident where I had not finished bolting the roof down properly and one of the roofing panels got caught in the wind and folded over on itself, but fortunately this went back in place with only the slightest distortion.

Planning is a good starting point, but be prepared to redesign as needed, and it might be a good idea to source parts you are going to use before you get too far to go back.

GLAZING

Although we didn't go for the additional insulation, double-glazing was a good option for security, robustness and retaining some heat.

INSULATION

Insulating the roof and floor was an option. Both are easy to do. Reducing heat loss through the walls is primarily achieved through increasing the thickness of the wall logs (timber is a relatively good insulator).

Roof insulation, for this type of cabin, is installed on top of the timber roof deck and is then covered by the roofing membrane. This method of construction is called a 'warm roof' as the roof structure itself is on the warm side of the insulation. It is therefore more protected against condensation.

The floor insulation is installed beneath the timber floor. However, as this cabin was to be used as a gym, people would be getting warm through exercise, so keeping the building warm was not a priority. Insulation would have been selected if the building was to be used as an office or music practice room, for example.

2. Installing the base

Materials
- 12 No. QuickJacks
- 4 x 2 timber
- 75mm-long annular ring shank nails
- Simpson joist hangers
- 30mm x 3.75 twisted galvanised nails

Tools required
- Set square
- 8m tape
- Carpenter's pencil
- Saw
- Drill/driver

▲ Adjustable metal screw jacks.

▼ The proposed adjustable shed base frame.

Using an adjustable metal screw jack system

A common feature of many shed-building projects is that the new structure is to be built on an old patio and doesn't quite fit. To avoid the time and expense of ripping up the old patio and to create a decent base with good airflow underneath the building, we chose to use a system of adjustable metal screw jacks to support the building.

The advantages of using a system such as this are:

- The jacks cope easily with a sloping base, avoiding the need for cutting of firring timbers or lots of small packing pieces
- They also cope easily with bearing on to a variety of materials, including the old patio and some newly constructed individual bases
- The jacks raise the base of the shed off the wet ground, which allows good airflow beneath the shed and keeps the base timbers dry
- Wire mesh can be installed around the base of the shed to stop pets or unwanted wild animals (foxes or rats) taking up residence.

The project started, as always, with creating a design so that we could work out the right quantities of materials needed. I combined the information from the cabin supplier and jack supplier to create the design to support the timber floor bearers and perimeter walls of the cabin.

The sequence of construction was dictated by the installation instructions provided by the jack supplier. These were fairly minimal – an A4 sheet with a few words and pictures – so we have expanded on them here to give you our own experience, as well as a few pitfalls to avoid.

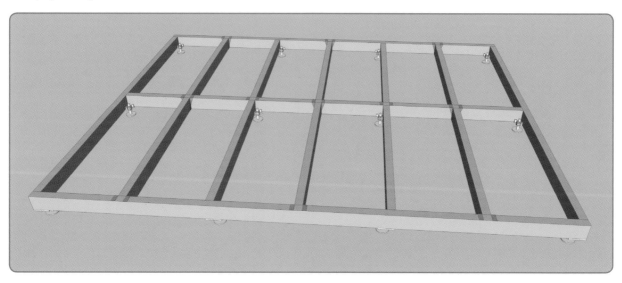

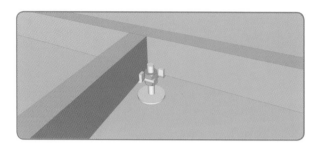

▲ Connection at screw jack location.

▶ Frame junction without jack.

START BY BUILDING THE BASE FRAME

We used two different types of connection:

a) At the connections where jacks occurred we used two 75mm ring shank nails skew nailed to secure the members together. These joints were supported from beneath by the screw jacks, which were secured to the timbers by two screws from beneath and two screws into the sides of the timber

b) At connections where jacks didn't occur, we used Simpson joist hangers.

ATTACH THE BRACKET SUPPORT PLATES TO THE FRAME

These plates are 8mm thick and heavy duty. The bolt that forms the screw jack is 24mm diameter, so it is all robust stuff.

The brackets are fitted to the underside of the frame using two of the supplied screws and then another two screws are used to fix into the sides through the folded-up section of the plate.

▼ Fixing the bracket support plate. Two screws into sides of members and two screws into the underside.

▶ Screw adjuster installed into bracket support plate. Note: upper locknut is left intentionally high at this point.

ATTACH THE ADJUSTERS

The adjusters are a flat plate with a nut welded to it and a 150mm-long piece of 24mm diameter threaded rod. This forms the jack body. A lower adjustment nut is threaded onto the jack and the assembly is then passed through the large hole in the bracket. The upper nut is a locknut, which is tightened once the whole frame has been levelled.

At this point, the lower nut is set about 10mm off the lowest point on the jack.

FLIP THE FRAME OVER SO THAT THE FRAME IS SITTING ON THE JACKS

For this project, the base extended off the patio. Also, none of the boundaries of the garden were square to each other. One of the benefits of building a shed in this way is that, once constructed, the location of the base can be moved to suit. In this case, we left plenty of space around the edge of the shed for access during construction and future maintenance.

Also, leaving space between the shed and the fence gives the wood a chance to dry out and minimises the potential

▼ The adjustable shed base frame. The left hand and rear jacks are on the six new bases. Three of the front row and the next row back are on the existing patio.

▲ Construction of new support pad with standard paving slab with post mix concrete beneath.

▲ Working around the base ensuring all perimeter beams are level. Note: Intermediate jacks not touching the ground at this point.

for timber decay. Building a shed too close to a fence is not advisable.

We then found that we needed to construct six pad bases where the jacks didn't land on the patio.

ADJUST THE LOWER NUT TO LEVEL
Levelling of the shed should start at the corner where the ground is highest. The frame should be supported on the four corner jacks. All intermediate jacks should be raised up out of the way.

Using a spirit level, work from one corner to the next. Adjust the next corner jack so that the spirit level bubble is central. When you get back to the corner where you started, all sides should be level. However, you may need another circuit to undertake the fine adjustment.

▼ Start levelling at the corner where the ground is highest.

Now lower all the intermediate and internal jacks to the ground. Check that all of the timbers are still level.

TIGHTEN THE UPPER LOCKING NUT
This prevents any changes in adjustment over time. As this shed is reasonably heavy – it has 45mm-thick solid timber walls – we didn't need to fix the bases to the ground.

If it had been a lightweight timber, metal or PVC shed, we would have used either a resin anchor or a self-tapping concrete screw to secure the base to the concrete paving slabs.

With the shed base complete, the next step was to start building the log cabin.

▼ Intermediate jacks in position and locknut tightened.

3. Constructing the side walls

The cabin was delivered on a rigid-bodied truck. The client paid a small extra charge to have the cabin unloaded and the parts carried to the end of the garden. The alternative was to have the timber (approximately 1 tonne) offloaded at the kerb side and carry the parts to site ourselves….

In addition to saving the carrying of parts, the unloading was useful as the driver and his mate knew what they had to offload and stacked the structural components on timber bearers near the pre-prepared base. The more fragile elements such as windows, double-glazed units, doors and trim were stacked in a covered store. These parts were needed later in the build, so having them kept separately protected them from potential water or accidental damage.

▲ Truck delivering parts to site.

▲ Main timber parts stacked and protected adjacent to build site.

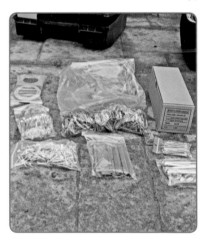

▲ Bags of screws and hardware.

▲ Fragile parts stored under cover in shed to side of house.

Fixing the timber bearers in place

The first step to assembling the cabin was to find the treated timber bearers that were to support the floor. We fixed these in place with a screw at each cross location. The recommended construction sequence is not to install the floorboards until later. This has the benefit that you don't end up with lots of muddy footprints on the floor. However, it does keep you fit, high-stepping over all those joists!

▶ Base with floor bearers installed. Checking for level with spirit level.

▲ General view of the first course of timber logs.

◄ Getting started with the walls.

▼ Detail of interlocking logs at a corner.

Starting the walls

The walls of this cabin are made from a series of 45 x 100mm interlocking planks. The top and bottom surfaces of the 'logs' are grooved so that they interlock. The ends of each log are notched so that they lock with logs coming in from adjoining walls. Make sure that you sort out the different lengths of log and count the number of each.

To start the wall off, we placed half a log at the front and the back of the cabin. Then we secured the log to the base with a long screw. The two logs at the front are only part lengths that are the start of the opening for the door.

Then we added logs in the alternate direction. This process can be done alone or with assistance. The logs themselves weigh approximately 10kg for a 4m length, and so are quite light, but they can be a bit unwieldy, so having an assistant is a bonus.

One factor highlighted in the assembly instructions is that timber is a natural material and is susceptible to warp, bow and split. I found the timber for this cabin to be of very good quality, although some of the logs did have significant bends along their length.

With logs that aren't perfectly straight, some 'encouragement' is required to get them to interlock. You can use a rubber mallet or a steel lump hammer with a timber block to 'tap' on top of the logs to get them into place. We chose to use a 4lb lump hammer and a short

▲ View of second course of logs.

▼ Detail of second course of logs at a corner.

section of timber. This applied plenty of force to the logs, but the wood distributed it along the top of the log so that we didn't damage any of the interlocking grooves.

If you choose to use a rubber mallet, make sure that you buy the non-marking kind. These are made of a white-coloured rubber and won't leave black marks on the logs.

The amount of bend in each log was different, but we found that the majority bound together well. Only a few needed additional taps from the hammer to fully interlock.

Once the walls have been started, check them horizontally and vertically for level every couple of courses of logs with your spirit level. This will ensure that if there are any problems you spot them and correct them before the building goes too far out of plumb.

Keep on stacking the logs until you reach the window sill.

▼ 4lb hammer and timber block, with logs interlocked.

4. Installing the window and door frames

▲ Window and door frames located prior to building up the walls.

One of the benefits of this design of cabin is the flexibility of location of the side window. It is easy to put the window in either side wall and then decide to have the window towards the front or rear of the cabin. We opted to have the window in the front corner of the cabin towards the sunniest aspect of the building to give it a lighter and more outdoorsy feel.

Looking first at the window frame

The window frame was supplied prefabricated, whereas the door frame came supplied in three parts. The logs were tied in to the side of the frames with clips to give the walls some continuity.

▲ The window frame, prior to installation.

◀ Corner of window frame.

The window had a central frame of timber that was the same width as the wall. Flat timbers had been screwed to the front and back so there was a rebate all around the frame. The window was simply lifted into position over the pre-assembled logs.

We tied the window into the logs either side at two points on each of the uprights. The detail of the tie was important as it holds the window in position side to side but allows the window and wall to move different amounts vertically as the logs expand and contract.

The metal ties were made out of two pieces of

▲ Log connection to window frame, allowing the logs to move vertically while aligning them.

interlocking metal. We screwed one piece to the end of a log abutting the frame and the other to the window frame. The log was then placed in position – it is important that the tie on the end of the log engages with the tie on the window frame.

In addition to the window frame ties holding the wall together, the timbers on the front and the back of the frame keep the logs aligned vertically. Without the straightening help from the window frame, there is difficulty in getting the wall to be vertical.

Installation and assembly of the door frame

The door frame is large, so it was supplied in three parts: two uprights and a cross piece. You should lay out the pieces on the shed floor so that the corners can be interlocked. The frame on this model is held together and stiffened by two steel corner plates. These plates are vital to helping the cabin resist the side loads from wind on the shed. Before screwing the corner plates in position, we measured from corner to corner of the door frame to

▲ Connection of door components. Upright to cross piece.

make sure that the frame was square. The corners are right angles when the two diagonal measurements are the same.

When the frame has been made square and locked in place with the corner plates, it can be lifted in to place. This operation needs two people and the frame is lifted up and over the two small wing walls, and gently lowered into place. Check again that both uprights are vertical and that they haven't been moved during lifting.

As you keep on constructing the walls, add in ties in a similar way to the windows. Ties are needed at the quarter points of the wall.

You can now continue stacking the logs up until you get to the top of the door and window frame.

▲ The door frame complete and installed.

► Corner plates fixed in position.

► Ties between logs and door frame.

▼ Logs stacked to full height of door frame.

5. Roof framing

The roof of the cabin was formed from timber purlins spanning 4m from one side of the cabin to the other. The pitch of the roof was formed by notches cut in to the side wall timbers.

One problem that we came across in constructing the roof was that the upper level of the side walls was supplied as one piece with all of the timbers joined together. This made the section very heavy and it was also impossible to get the corners to interlock with the intersecting walls.

After a bit of head scratching, we determined that the bottom timber was screwed into place with a very large screw. The screw could be removed to release the bottom timber. This enabled the corners to interlock. It also made the remaining section of side wall lighter and easier to lift in to place.

With the side walls in place, the purlins were lifted onto the top of the walls. The purlins slotted over the walls, tying

▼ The large gable pieces were slightly problematic as they were very heavy.

▲ Gable pieces in place with purlins spanning between the walls.

▲ Washer spacer to ensure 2mm gap between roof boards.

the eaves together at precisely the correct spacing. Two people were needed for lifting the purlins into place. Some of the purlins needed a bit of encouragement with the hammer and spacer so that they sat correctly.

The roof deck, on top of the purlins, was formed from 20mm-thick boards, 100mm wide. These had a maximum span of 700mm. **Care is needed when working at heights and especially on partially constructed roofs.** The roof boards were fixed using step ladders for access, as the instructions rightly warned not to walk on the roof until it was fully complete.

The roof boards were fixed in place using 40mm ring shank nails with one nail at each intersection of board and purlin. The first board was aligned with the groove pointing outwards and in line with the end of the purlin.

The boards interlocked with a tongue and groove to form a single timber sheet for the cabin roof. To accommodate future expansion and contraction of the boards, a 2mm gap between the edges of the boards was recommended by the supplier. Two washers made a good guide for this at the start of fixing the boards, but as work progressed it became increasingly easy to judge the gap by eye with occasional checks with a tape measure to make sure that one end of the roof wasn't 'creeping' ahead of the other.

We chose to use a hammer to drive the nails. A nail gun was an option, but for a relatively small roof such as this, the

▼ Edge roof board, before being cut flush with edge of purlin.

time saved would have been offset by the time spent going to the hire shop to collect and then return the tool, as well as the cost of hire and the additional nails. In this case, we were right to rely on the trusty hammer.

We needed to fix the last roof board at the far side of the roof from where we started. The position of this board couldn't be determined in advance and so the last board to be placed had to be cut. We put the board in position and marked the cut line flush with the ends of the supporting purlins at each end. Then we drew a pencil line between the two points using a surplus floorboard. The cut is most easily made using a circular saw.

With the roof deck in position, the finishing touches were made to it. At the front and rear this meant fitting timber battens to the edge of the roof so that we could fix the roof trim. Along the bottom of the roof slopes, to the front and rear of the shed, a batten was fixed to the underside of the roof boards and a vertical batten was screwed on to this. The roof membrane was fitted over the top of this.

On the gable sides of the shed a trim member is made up by screwing together a board and batten. This is then painted and put to one side. This section of trim is fitted once the roof membrane has been installed.

The next stage was to install the roof membrane.

▲ The batten to enable fixing of roof trim.

▼ The roof trim to gable ends. This is to be painted and fixed in place after the roof membrane is installed.

6. Installing the roof membrane

Many people are used to repairing and replacing their shed roof with traditional shed felt, so using a new type of roof-covering system can be a bit daunting. Here is a step-by-step guide to EPDM roofing to show how easy it actually is to install.

Materials
- Roll of EPDM roofing
- Adhesive
- Drip edging

Tools required
- Paint roller
- Paint tray
- Scissors

We recommend buying the roofing and adhesive from the same supplier. This way you know that the two will work together, as the adhesive needs to bond to both a timber deck and the rubber. The adhesive is not anything super high-tech, but don't use some PVA glue that you have lying around just to save a few pennies.

At 1mm, EPDM roofing for a shed seems fairly thin. Thicker grades – 1.2 or 1.5mm – are used on industrial buildings, as these areas can be subject to foot traffic over the years.

When you order EPDM it is supplied in one large sheet, so you will need to work out the area of your roof. Allow for a 150mm overhang of material on each edge (so add 300mm to the overall dimension). Also allow for the slope of the roof and edge overhangs. The slope dimension is greater than the building dimension measured on plan.

> When you have a close look at the sheet that is delivered you will see that it is actually made up of a series of sheets (approx. 1.2m wide). The joints are factory bonded. It is difficult to spot these joints and for all practical purposes, they can be ignored.

Make sure that your roof is ready to receive the EPDM

Before loading your materials onto the roof, make sure that the roof is clean and dry. Also check that the temperature is likely to remain above 5°C for the next 24 hours. In addition,

▲ Roofing membrane laid out on clean and dry roof deck.

ensure that all nails and screws have been driven below the surface of the roof deck.

We completed the roof deck on this shed in the middle of December in the UK. It was raining as we finished nailing on the last roofing boards. It then froze that night. We spent the next couple of days getting the roof to dry out in the weak, mid-winter sun. We were lucky that we then hit a dry spell and the weather warmed up enough for us to bond the roof with the expectation that the temperature would remain above 7°C that night.

Lay the membrane out flat on the roof to double check that you've calculated the size correctly.

▼ Membrane on roof prior to bonding. The membrane overhangs the roof on all edges.

Bond the membrane to the roof deck

The roof was 3.5 x 4m with a relatively shallow roof slope. It was asymmetrical, the front cantilevered section relatively short in comparison to the longer slope at the rear. The shallow slope meant that we felt comfortable walking on the roof to install the membrane.

We started to bond the short front section of the roof first. To do this we folded back the front section of the roof

▲ Glue and roller, ready to start the application of adhesive.

membrane and started the glue application process by pouring a good dollop of glue into the paint tray.

The glue loaded well on to the roller and it was easy to get an even layer over the whole front section of roof (approx. 1.2 x 3.5m). We then flipped back the section of the membrane that we had folded back onto the glued area. We smoothed out the membrane over the glued section using a 'soft' broom. This got rid of any air bubbles between the deck and the membrane. Also, the pressure from the brush helped to create contact between the membrane and the roof, so increasing the bond between the two.

▼ Application of glue to the front section of roof.

▲ Ready to start the application of glue to the rear section.

With the front section complete, we repeated the process for the rear slope of the shed.

The rear slope was about 3m long, so we covered this in three sections of about a metre each. After each section, we unrolled the membrane over the glued area and repeated the smoothing with the soft broom.

For the last section, we started applying glue from the opposite side from where we had the ladder (we didn't want to paint ourselves into a corner!). When we had finished applying the glue we carefully walked on top of the freshly laid section of membrane. We could then fold the last section of the membrane into place and smooth it with the brush.

▼ Unfolding the membrane over the glued rear section of the roof.

▲ Completed section of rear roof, with yellow brush handle visible.

▲ The roof with timber side fascia fixed, ready to start fixing front trim.

Final checks for creases and air bubbles

For this project, the roof deck was made of individual tongue-and-groove timber planks about 100mm wide. Having the grooves in the roof deck stopped any significant air bubbles forming, as any trapped air could escape along the groove.

Just to emphasise again that this membrane is amazing in how strong and flexible it is. There is very little chance of creases forming in a small roof such as this.

With the membrane bonded to the deck, we got ready to fix the fascia and drip edge/trim around the perimeter of the roof. Before starting to fix the first section of trim, we pinned back the sections of the membrane at the corners and ridge. We used a small clout nail to hold the membrane in position.

▼ Corner with membrane pinned back prior to fixing side fascia.

This only needed to be temporary, as the edge trim would effectively hold the edge of the membrane in place.

Fix the side fascia first

The side fascia was made of two timber sections screwed together and painted. The fascia was fixed using wood screws to the end of the purlins that project through the wall. The screws passed through the EPDM membrane, clamping it between the end of the purlin and the fascia. These (and the ones fixing the front trim) were the only holes made in the membrane. As the holes were limited in number, outside of the main roof (in the overhang) and on a vertical surface, they were extremely unlikely to contribute to any future roof leak.

The front trim was fixed after the two sides had been secured.

The front trim doubles as a 'drip edge'

Water flows down the roof and drains off the roof on the front and back edge. The trim for this was formed using a two-part plastic drip edge. The back part of the trim was nailed to the roof edge beneath the membrane. The front part was then nailed to the roof with the nail passing through the roof membrane and the back part of the trim.

▼ Components of the front drip edge. Smaller nails are for fixing the rear part of the drip edge. Larger nails with plastic caps are for fixing main drip edge. The small black plastic piece is the cover piece for the joints in the trim.

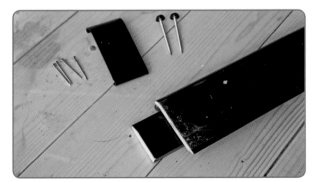

◄ Demonstration of how front and rear section of trim fix together. The membrane is sandwiched between the two pieces.

► The front trim, before removal of excess membrane.

The nails have ring shanks for improved pull-out resistance and have a plastic cap to give a neat appearance.

The trim came in 3m lengths and so we used one full piece and a short infill piece. There was a clip-on joining piece to cover the joint.

The last part of installing the EPDM membrane was to cut off the excess rubber membrane around the perimeter.

Remove the excess membrane around the roof perimeter

We first tried doing this with a Stanley craft knife. This struggled to cut the membrane, which once again shows how tough this EPDM material is. We ended up using the scissors that had been supplied by Rubber For Roofs, who supplied the whole kit (they know what works!).

Summary

The whole installation process was very quick and the end result looked extremely neat. The process didn't require any special skills or equipment. The roofing system impressed us

▲ The front trim, after removal of excess membrane.

so much that we will be using it to reroof a couple of our own sheds whose existing felt roofs have given up the ghost.

With the roof on and waterproof it was now time to start on finishing the building envelope.

▼ The completed roof.

7. Glazing the windows and installing the doors

Glazing the windows

The window frame was fitted as part of the main structure and supplied without the glazing fitted. All that remained was to install the double-glazed units that had been carefully put to one side with other more fragile items at the time of delivery.

▲ The window, prior to glazing.

There were two options to select from when the cabin was bought. These were either 4mm single-glazed windows or a double-glazed option. For this project, the double-glazed option was chosen, but the installation procedure was the same for both. The glazing was sized to have a 5mm gap around the perimeter. This gap was adjusted for tolerances using supplied plastic shims to support the glass

▼ The glazing components.

at the bottom and space the glass off the sides of the window frame.

The double-glazing was secured in place with pre-cut and nicely mitred glazing beads. The nails for these beads were extra thin to avoid splitting the timber.

The window installation was completed by running a

▲ The glazing beads in position.

bead of clear silicone sealant around the junction between the glass and the window frame. This bead minimises water getting into the frame. However, if significant water did start to get in to the cavity around the glazing, there were some pre-drilled holes in the bottom of the frame to allow it to escape.

▶ The glazing beads in place. Silicone sealant is applied to the outside of the window.

◄ Window with 'Georgian bars'.

► Connection of Georgian bars to window frame.

Some additional 'Georgian bars' were also supplied to give the cabin a matching look to your house, if that is what you prefer.

Installing the doors

In contrast to the windows, the doors came ready glazed. The doors for this cabin were of the bifold variety. This means that each leaf of the door folds in half and so it is quite easy to almost fully open up the front of the shed to make the most of fresh air in good weather.

The doors were supported on 'knuckles' that were screwed in to pre-drilled holes in the door frame uprights. There were three knuckles for each door, simply screwed in to position. Make sure that the knuckles align vertically before lifting the doors into position.

The doors were heavy and hinged in the centre of each leaf. They definitely needed two people working together to lift them into place: one doing the lifting and the other the aligning. It also helped to stack some wood up beneath the

door so that it was at just about the right height before the final lift into place.

With one door in place, it was a simple repeat for the other door. Then the moment of truth – did the doors align with

► Knuckle forming door hinge.

▼ Bifold doors in place before painting.

▲ Sliding bolt at top of door.

▲ Sliding bolt at bottom of door.

▼ Door handle with Euro lock.

each other and close? There were Allen key bolts on the hinges for raising and lowering the door and similar on the other part for minor adjustments to help the doors close.

Next, we fitted the bolts to secure the bifold doors to the door frame in the closed position. These were small sliding bolts at the top and bottom for each of the bifold hinge positions, with one set of bolts for the door that generally remains static.

The last step was to fit the door handle and Euro lock. This part was very straightforward.

With the doors and windows installed, the building envelope was complete and the building was weathertight.

▼ The doors in place after painting.

8. Installing the floor and internal fittings

▲ Material stacked inside the shed ready for the floor installation.

We left the floor until the cabin was watertight so that the planks would remain clean, dry and free from muddy footprints.

Installing the floorboards and skirting

Installation of the floorboards was similar to the roof, starting at one side of the cabin and working across to the opposite side. We drove in one nail per intersection between floorboard and floor bearer, leaving a 2mm gap between the edges of the boards to allow for expansion and contraction.

The main difference it had with the roof was that the nails in the floor were driven down an extra couple of mm below the floor level. This was to allow any sanding and to prevent anything catching on any slightly raised nail heads. As with the roof, the last floorboard would generally be cut to accommodate a final tolerance gap. However, for this particular cabin we were lucky, and the last board fitted perfectly.

The perimeter of the floor was neatened up and small gaps closed by installing a small skirting around the perimeter of the floor. A nice touch.

▼ Hammer and nail punch for driving nail heads below surface of floor.

▼ Installing the low height timber skirting.

▲ Pre-drilled hole for ventilation at top of gable wall.

▶ Ventilation hole with vent cover fitted.

Ventilating the building

Ventilation of small buildings can be a problem dependent on the local climate, building orientation and use. In an attempt to head off potential issues, this cabin had two vent holes pre-drilled at the top of each gable. To prevent driven rain from getting in, the external side of the hole had a plastic vent cover with slats oriented downwards. In addition, with the hole located under the eaves, the probability of rain getting in was low. On the internal face another plastic cover was provided. This had a metal gauze insect screen to keep out unwanted visitors.

Fitting the roof ties

The last of the internal fittings were the roof ties. We bolted

these timber straps to the timbers at the top log and the bottom log.

When installed, the bolt was in the middle of the slot. This allowed the logs room to expand and contract without breaking the tie. The bolt was tightened to a sliding fit.

The purpose of these ties is to stop the roof being lifted off in strong winds. As you will have noted, the construction of the cabin did not require any nails or screws to hold it together. It relied solely on the interlocking logs. So in theory, in strong winds, the roof could be pulled off. The purpose of the straps is to mobilise the whole weight of the building to stop this happening.

Installing the ties was the last task in the construction of the building structure. But this did not mean that building the cabin was complete…

▼ Four roof ties were required, one in each corner.

▲ Top of roof tie.

▼ Slotted hole at bottom of roof tie.

9. Finishing works

With the shed kit fully erected, there were still a few items that needed to be added to complete the build. We painted the roof trim and Georgian window bars with a water-repellent timber stain before fixing them in place. Then we gave the rest of the shed two coats of the same liquid to give it 3 to 4 years of protection.

Other items to complete the build included adding a mesh around the bottom of the shed to stop pets and other animals from escaping or taking up residence there. Having a mesh also allows air ventilation, enabling moisture from the ground to disperse and stops the base timbers from getting wet.

We dug a drainage trench at the back of the shed to act as a soakaway for water draining off the rear of the roof, lining it with landscaping fabric and filling it with gravel. The gravel allows the water to drain away and also reduces 'bounce back' from rain soaking the base of the shed. The landscaping fabric stops the gravel getting mixed with the clay soil beneath.

With the shed raised up from the surrounding ground, a step helps to make access to the shed easier. This is easily

built out of decking boards and some offcuts of timber. When building the steps, aim to make the risers equal and give each going at least 225mm to minimise the possibility of tripping.

The final thing to do was to install the gym equipment and get fit!

> **Ongoing maintenance**
>
> ■ Check for drainage issues and wood that is regularly getting damp – install guttering to capture rain and divert into a water butt or flower bed
> ■ Check the roof for damage or deterioration of roof covering
> ■ Recoat the cabin with preservative – the time period for this is dependent upon type of preservative used (three to five years).

▼ Completed cabin in summer.

71

SHED 2: 8 X 6 SHED

1. Overview

A classic 8 x 6ft shed is a useful size for many uses, from the storage of garden tools to a garden office or even a pub shed. The time, detail and materials put in to this shed mean that it will most likely end up as an office or leisure building.

Materials and methods used

Here is a quick rundown of the materials and methods used for this project.

FOUNDATIONS

The foundations for this shed are our favourite way of creating a level shed base while minimising the amount of groundwork required. Pad foundations, adjustable screw jacks with a timber floor frame are a simple and economic way of supporting a shed.

▲ View of almost-completed shed.

FRAME

Although the cost of timber for the frame of a shed isn't one of the biggest cost items on the list (the roofing material and cladding are number 1 and 2 for this build), it is always good to save a bit of cash where you can. So we used some 4 x 2ft rafters that we salvaged from a building refurbishment. Often, builders are happy to give these materials away, as it saves them the time and cost of disposal.

FLOOR

The floor of the building is built on a 'deck' made from 4 x 2in joists. The structural floor is made from shuttering ply. This material is strong and relatively waterproof. It is cheaper

◀ Screw jacks were used to support the shed base.

▶ Section through salvaged 4 x 2 timber on the left comparing it to some shop-bought 2 x 2 timber on the right.

► Comparison of the different finishes on formply.

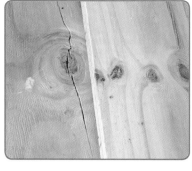

than many forms of plywood, as it has one smooth side (which is used uppermost) and a rough side (which is used facing downwards). Other finishing materials, such as carpet, tiles or wood flooring, could be used on top of this decking for those requiring a higher class of finish.

▲ Trial assembly of the hipped roof.

ROOF

For this project, we opted to go for one of the more complex roof styles, a 'hipped' roof. The reason for this was to present an idea of the variety of things that can

▲ Close-up of sweet chestnut shake roof.

fairly easily be achieved and also to highlight some of the issues that come with a more complex shape. In terms of roof covering for this project, we threw in something quite challenging: sweet chestnut shakes. Splitting roof tiles from raw logs and then shaping them into individual roof tiles is hard, time-consuming work, but leads to a beautiful and very individual roof.

SIDING

As we planned to put a lot of effort into the roof and roofing material, we also considered how to approach the siding. We chose to use Douglas fir feather edge boards, but rather than apply a coat of waterproof stain or oil we wanted to experiment with a technique called Shou Sugi Ban. This is an old Japanese method of wood preserving (normally used on

▲ Trialling Shou Sugi Ban finish for the siding.

cedar wood) that involves charring the surface of the wood, brushing off the excess charred surface and then coating the wood with decking oil. This technique brings out the beautiful grain of the wood and gives it a beautiful colour and patina, as well as giving the siding a long life.

WINDOWS AND DOOR

Not having given ourselves an easy time for the main part of the project, we continued this theme by making our own door, using planks cut from waney edge boards, and making simple window frames to use with some recycled double-glazed units (continuing the recycling theme from the shed frame).

Finally, as a finishing touch to the door, we created a simple home-made door latch from some of the sweet chestnut timber we had left over.

▲ Completed door installed on shed.

► View of 'skeleton' of 8 x 6 shed.

2. Preparing the base

PLAN OF BASE

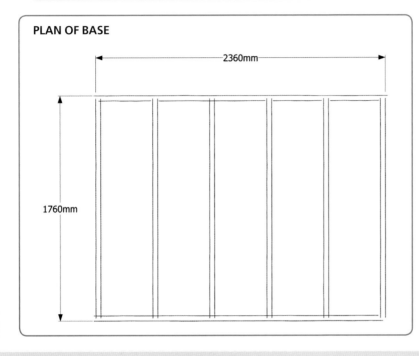

2360mm

1760mm

The base for this shed is a bit like a table top. It is supported on screw jacks on each corner. This means that the timber forming the shed base is not in contact with the ground. Although it will get a bit damp occasionally, it won't be continually damp.

Also, having only four points of support, making a foundation uses significantly less material than creating a whole concrete base for the shed. The cost of this in comparison to a more traditional base formed of small timber bearers is that you spend a bit more on timber but spend significantly less time and money on creating a level concrete base. As well as saving you money on the initial build, this has a benefit

Pocket hole joints

The connection system that we chose for connecting the framework for the shed base, and also the frame to the shed, is a heavy-duty pocket hole joint. The benefit is that each joint is quickly made. If a member needs to move, then it can easily be done. Creating joints in this way is also stronger than the more traditional method of screwing the joints in place or skew nailing them. Once you have this relatively inexpensive kit you will find all sorts of other construction and repair jobs around the house that you can use it for.

Pocket hole joints are simply made with a jig, drill bit,

driver and pocket hole screws. The central part of the kit is a jig that clamps to one end of the timber that is being connected. A collar on a stepped drill bit is set to the length advised in the instructions. The stepped drill bit is required, as the larger diameter section of the drill creates the hole for the head of the screw, while the smaller diameter section creates the hole for the shank of the screw.

The jig is made dimensionally so that the drill enters the wood at the correct angle and a hole is created at the correct distance from the end of the timber. For this project, two heavy-duty screws were used for each connection.

▼ Heavy-duty pocket hole jig kit.

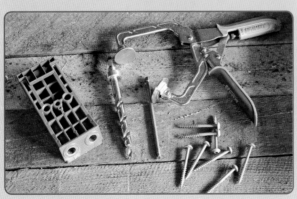

▼ Drilling the holes for the pocket hole screws.

down the line when you want to move house and take
the shed with you or if you want to remodel the garden
and don't fancy having to demolish a heavy concrete
slab or patio.

Creating the timber frame

The first step in creating the shed base is to cut the timbers
to length: two for the sides and six in between. The
perimeter timbers are laid out to form a rectangle
supported on lengths of timber. The frame is 'squared-up'
by measuring across the diagonals. The two diagonal
measurements need to be identical. We used a webbing
ratchet strap to clamp the timbers together and hold them
in close contact while we inserted and tightened the
pocket hole screws. The intermediate timbers were then
fixed in place using the same ratchet strap to hold the
frame tightly together.

▲ Perimeter timbers in place and checking the diagonals.

▼ Using a webbing ratchet strap to hold the timbers in place before
making the connection with pocket hole screws.

◄ Close-up of
installing the
pocket hole
screws.

► View of base
prior to installing
'noggins'.

▲ Jack support socket.

▲ Jack support socket with jack in place.

Fixing the noggins

With the frame assembled, timber blocking (known as 'noggins') are fixed between the timbers at 1200mm from one of the long edges. The purpose of these noggins is to provide support to the edge of the plywood decking used for the floor. If a specific flooring ply that had a tongue and groove created in the edge had been used then noggins are not specifically needed. But having them there gives the structure extra rigidity and support.

Before fixing the floor decking, bolt in place the jack support sockets with the hole adjacent to the edge timber. The reason

▼ Underside of shed base with noggins in place to support the edges of the ply floor.

for this is so that the load is transferred from the jack end plate directly into the timber. The two bolts help to stabilise the timber but are only there to hold the timber in place.

The last picture shows the underside of the completed base. The noggins and jacks are in place and the plywood deck is screwed in place.

Levelling the base

The last step is to level the base by adjusting the nut on the screw jacks. Start at one corner and work your way round the perimeter using a 900mm long spirit level, levelling each edge in turn.

You now have a level base on which to start constructing other elements of the shed such as the roof, walls and door.

3. Building the roof

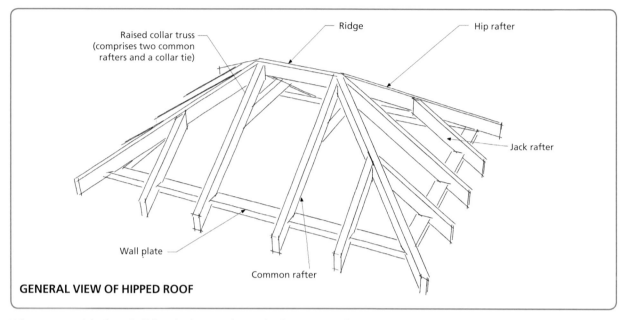

Raised collar truss (comprises two common rafters and a collar tie)

Ridge

Hip rafter

Jack rafter

Common rafter

Wall plate

GENERAL VIEW OF HIPPED ROOF

Why move straight from building the base to the roof? The answer to that question is that it so much easier to get things right while working at ground level. For a small roof such as this, getting the roof right and then taking it apart to reassemble at high level once the walls have been built is a

▲ Rafter with marking tools and cutting dimensions.

▼ Using a mitre saw to cut compound rafter angles.

small price to pay. The alternative is lots of trips up and down a step ladder measuring, checking and fitting the rafters.

The overall base dimensions are the same as the overall dimensions at the top of the walls, so moving the pre-constructed roof up to the next level is a fairly straightforward operation.

We chose to build this hipped roof as it shows all of the processes that you need if you want to build simpler roofs such as a gable or mono-pitch roof. So let's get started…

The roof is the most dimension-critical element of the frame. There are angles, dimensions and compound angles to contend with.

The main components of this roof are the rafters, ridge piece, hip rafters and jack rafters. We produced a 'Sketch up' model of the roof, and for a small roof it is not difficult to print out dimensions for each member. Roof carpenters who do this day in and day out use a roofing square and have techniques for making the cutting of rafters, 'birdsmouths' and compound angles relatively straightforward. But these techniques take a while to master, so it is easier for a one-off job to stick with measured dimensions and angles.

Cutting the rafters

We would recommend that you use a mitre saw for cutting the rafters. It is quicker and you can easily replicate angles and dimensions, as well as cutting compound angles for the hip and jack rafters. Cutting these members by hand might feel authentic, but you really will get a much better job using a powered mitre saw.

Take a while to consider the lengths of timber that you have and how best to cut the lengths of rafters that you need so you minimise waste. Use a tape measure, set square

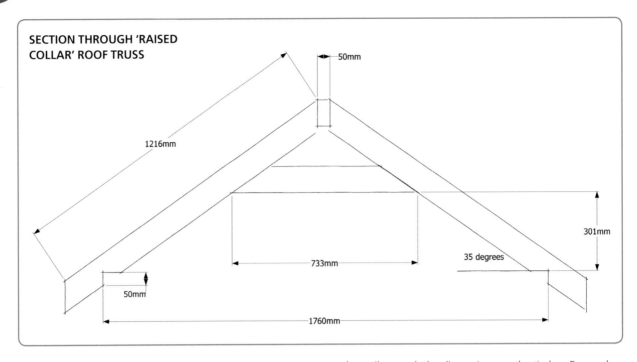

SECTION THROUGH 'RAISED COLLAR' ROOF TRUSS

50mm

1216mm

301mm

35 degrees

733mm

50mm

1760mm

▼ Birdsmouth at rafter foot.

and pencil to mark the dimensions on the timber. Remember the old saying, 'measure twice, cut once'. You will probably make at least one error in cutting and will need to think of a way around it.

We used a jig saw to cut out the 'birdsmouth' for the rafter feet. If you are good with a hand saw, then this would be another way to do it.

CUTTING THE COMMON RAFTERS AND RIDGE PIECE
The first members to cut are the common rafters and the ridge piece. These have simple lengths and dimensions (in contrast to the compound angles on the ends of the jack

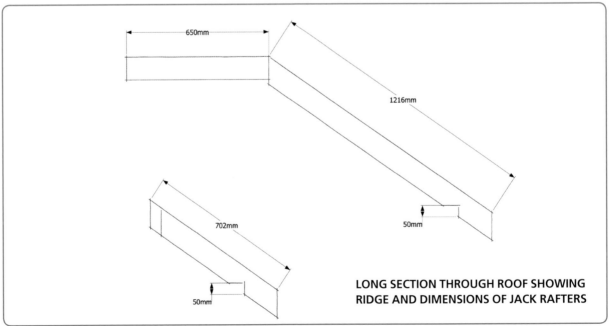

650mm

1216mm

702mm

50mm

50mm

LONG SECTION THROUGH ROOF SHOWING RIDGE AND DIMENSIONS OF JACK RAFTERS

rafters). We used pocket hole screws to make the connections, as we like the clean, uncluttered appearance and also how easy it was to take the roof apart once constructed.

Lay the rafters out on the frame bed, make the connections and then lift in to position. Make sure the rafter feet are central on the short edge and screw them into position. Adding the pair of rafters from each ridge point will stabilise the roof further. These lateral rafters also have what is known as a collar tie. This turns this pair of rafters into a raised collar truss, which adds to the strength of the roof.

CUTTING AND SHAPING THE HIP RAFTERS

The next step is to cut the hip rafters. In a more traditional roof, this member would be deeper than the main joists, but in a small roof such as this, when the timbers are of a short span, this wasn't felt necessary. Once again, work from figured dimensions to mark the cut lines with pencil. To make the cuts, you will need to rotate the mitre saw about the horizontal and vertical axis. All four of the hip rafters are identical. The rafters, hip rafters and ridge meet at a point. It is now that you will see how accurate your setting out and cutting has been.

▶ Laying the cut rafters out on the frame bed.

▲ Making the connection between rafters using pocket hole screws.

▼ Lifting the longitudinal frame upright.

▼▼ Starting to stabilise the frame with rafters.

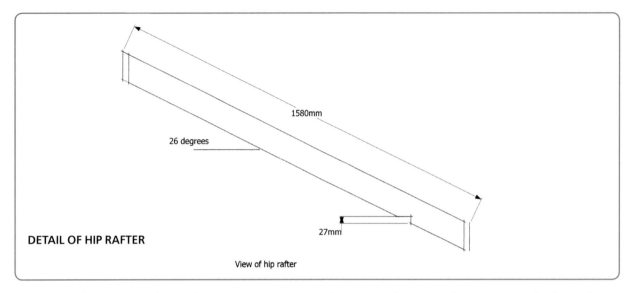

DETAIL OF HIP RAFTER

1580mm

26 degrees

27mm

View of hip rafter

The infill rafters have two designs that are similar but 'handed'. You will need to make sure that you rotate the saw in the alternative dimension to get the 'handed' version. If you are not clear on what 'handed' means, take a look at the end of the roof – both types of infill rafter have similar dimensions and birdsmouths. But when you cut these rafters, you will need to take extra care to rotate the saw in the opposite direction so that you get one that fits on the left-hand side and one on the right.

The hip rafters need additional shaping so that the roofing battens fit in a straight line. It is possible to introduce these bevels through cutting the rafter with a handheld circular saw, or planing the edge of the rafter with an electric or manual plane. We chose to use a manual plane as we really enjoy the sound and sensation of cutting the wood shavings to get the wood into the right shape.

FIXING THE RAFTERS IN PLACE

With the infill rafters cut and the hip rafters shaped, you can now fix the jack rafters in place. These are simply screwed through the bevel face of the rafter at the top end and into the base at the bottom end.

The roof structure is now complete. Take a moment to check that the roof lines up in each direction by sighting along the plane of the roof and along the bottom ends of the rafter.

You might even want to cut the roofing battens at this stage; however, we left that until later.

When you are satisfied that you have completed the roof, mark the joints. Having well-marked joints will make reassembling the roof on top of the walls a much simpler task.

▲ View of completed frame.

▼ Close-up of point where six rafters meet.

▼ Planing the hip rafters.

4. Adding side panels and bracing

▲ Laying out the timbers on the shed floor to form a wall panel.

The great thing about constructing the base first is that you have a level, clear space to use as a work area on which to construct the rest of the frame elements. The construction of the side panels continues in a very similar way to building the frame for the base.

The horizontal timbers for the top and bottom of the wall and the vertical wall studs are cut to length. The pocket holes (if that is the jointing method you choose) are drilled. The timbers are then set out on the shed floor to the required dimensions and checked for squareness. Whichever joining method you use, we recommend using the ratchet strap to hold the frame together while you make the connections.

Adding bracing

All sheds need some method of bracing to stabilise the frame against side forces such as wind. The main way that bracing works is by making triangles in the frame – an inherently stable shape, in contrast to rectangles, which start to lean and become 'lozenge' shaped when pushed from the side. Bracing is achieved through fixing timber members into the frame, using plywood as a 'skin' for the wall, or using another material entirely.

For this project we decided to experiment with using metal strapping. This material is very thin and only resists tension forces, so it needs to be installed in the form of a cross brace. As you will see later on, the experiment was not successful. When we put the roof on and pushed the

ELEVATION OF SIDE AND REAR WALL.

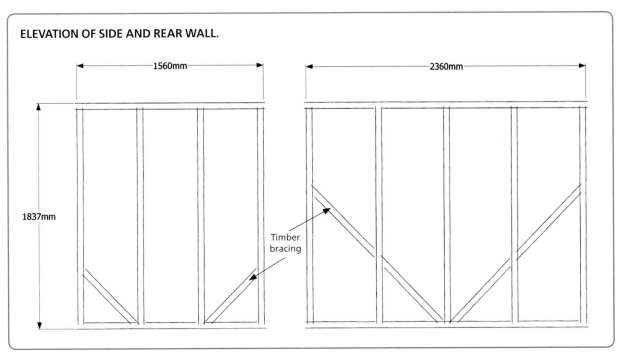

1560mm

2360mm

1837mm

Timber bracing

▲ The metal strapping experiment was not a success. The thin metal cross bracing straps were later replaced with timber braces attached into place with pocket screws to give a safer, more robust and visually attractive result.

▲ First wall panel coach screwed into position.

◄ Close-up of coach screw fixing.

▼ Constructing the second wall panel.

frame, it didn't fall over but neither did it feel particularly solid. The last straw was when we were fixing some siding and cut a knuckle on the sharp metal. The lack of solidity along with the safety aspect consigned metal strapping to the rubbish bin. The bracing of choice was 4x2 timbers screwed to the timber frame, see page 83.

Positioning the wall panels

As you make each wall panel, put them to one side until you have all four walls complete. The frames are then lifted into position. We bolted the frames down to the base frame using three 100mm long hex-head coach screws per panel. When you set out these fixings, make sure that you put them on the centre line of the member below. If you set them out on the centre line of the bottom plate of the wall you will just be bolting through the wall plate into the 18mm plywood decking.

The first wall panel that you put up should be stable by itself for a short period once you have three bolts holding it down. However, adding the second panel will start to add rigidity to the system. The second panel, if it is square, will make the adjoining panel vertical. The two panels can then be connected using the same bolts as for fixing down to the base.

The advantage of using the hex-head coach screws, rather than nails or Phillips head screws, is for the ease of dismantling if you ever need to move or modify the shed. We would recommend using three bolts at each interface: one at the top, one at the bottom and one in the middle. The middle bolt will help to make the member as straight as possible.

Once you have all four walls up, there are two jobs to do. Assemble the roof framework that you built earlier and install some additional 'nailers' to facilitate installation of the cladding.

Installing the roof framework

Installing the roof framework is the first part of working at height. Although this shed isn't very high, any fall from height has potential to cause injury, so make sure that your work platform is as stable as possible. We used a couple of step ladders – a smaller lighter one inside the shed that was easy to move round and a larger, taller ladder outside. This had a wider base which made it a lot more stable.

▼ All four walls in position. Note the clamps used to hold the wall joints together before installation of the screws.

When it comes to installing the roof, the larger the elements that you can lift in one piece, the less 'fiddling round' at height that you will have to do. As you can see from the picture, we kept the trusses in one piece along with the ridge member. This meant that we had a slightly heavier lift, but we didn't have to temporarily support the rafters while we installed the ridge and the collar joint. Both of these would have been very fiddly to install 'piece-wise'.

You can also see the ratchet strap that we used to pull the slight bow out of the top plate of the wall panels.

The two trusses and the ridge form the core of the roof support, and the feet of each member are then screwed down to the wall plate. The end rafters and the hip rafters can then be installed, followed by the jack rafters. Each rafter is secured to the wall plate at the base and the hip or ridge at its top end using a 100mm long No.5 screw.

Fitting the nailers to enable the cladding

Corner joints are a critical location for any shed. They form a break in the timber cladding and a connection point between panels. The corner joints need to be strong and weatherproof. The sketch on page 95 shows the arrangement of the corner detail.

For this project I opted to use a breathable membrane to cover the vertical joints in the panel and then to space off an additional corner member with spacers. This creates a three joist corner, which gives lots of places for securing the cladding on the outside. It also creates a good layout for fixing the lining to the shed internally, if that were to be required.

Before we go on to fix the cladding and roofing, a bit of fabrication needs to take place. For this shed, this will take the form of making the roofing material and preparing and cutting the cladding.

You can save a lot of time by using modern roofing materials, such as bitumen roofing shingles or EPDM for the roof. The same goes for the siding. Rather than opting for the charring and brushing, a simple coat of stain will quickly give the timber protection. We included the split sweet chestnut shakes and the Shou Sugi Ban siding to give you some extra options if you want to challenge yourself and make your shed more individual.

▼ The first two trusses in position.

▲ Completed roof structure.

▲ Detail at interface between panels.

▶ Interface with timber spacer block installed.

▼ Interface showing three spacer blocks and nailer piece about to be fixed.

5. Making roof shakes

John was originally going to use bitumen shingles for roofing this shed. However, after meeting Ben Law during the construction of the sweet chestnut barn and then reading and researching his work, he decided to give sweet chestnut shakes a try. He explains below how he went about it:

For most roofing projects you just buy the material and install it. For this project, I planned to create each part of the roof from its raw material.

The raw material for shakes is, of course, a log. There are two methods of splitting a log to create shakes. One is the 'quarter sawn method' and the second is 'through and through'. The best method to create quality shakes is the quarter sawn method.

Quarter sawn shakes are relatively stable and don't warp. The shakes are created from radial timber and have the growth rings as close as possible to right angles across the width of the shake. The only downside is that a relatively large-diameter log is required to cut them from. To achieve a shake width of between 100 and 125mm you will need a minimum of 350mm diameter log. Sweet chestnut is cut (coppiced) on a rotation of about 15–20 years with diameters of 200–250mm. So you will need to find a timber yard that can get you some timber that has been 'overstood', left for longer than the normal coppice rotation. The theoretical maximum number of shakes that you will get from a log of this size is 32, but due to imperfections in the

logs (branches, twist, etc.) and imperfections in your splitting technique (if you are a beginner like me) you will most likely average around 20 decent shakes per log.

It is possible to cut shakes from smaller diameter logs if you use the through and through method. I tried this method and ended up with more waste per log than the quarter sawn method. Also shakes split using this method tend to warp more with changes in moisture content. The central shakes have less tendency to split, but as growth rings pass through the log at a shallower angle, the movement becomes greater.

Sourcing sweet chestnut is probably easiest in the south-east of England, where it is commonly grown as coppiced timber and widely used for fencing materials. I sourced my logs from a very small timber yard that I found using a website set up to put small-time producers of woodland products in contact with small-time buyers: www.woodnet.org.uk/woodlots. The company I found, South East Oak Sawmills, were very friendly and in addition to locating some logs of the correct diameter, which were relatively branch free, they sawed them to the correct length too.

Oak is the other naturally durable timber occurring in temperate climates. Oak timbers have larger diameters than that of sweet chestnut, so you may not have the same difficulty in finding logs with sufficient diameter. However, the same problem of finding logs with straight, knot-free grain still apply, and it is only the oak heartwood that is really durable.

Comparison of splitting logs for shakes using the 'quarter sawn' vs the 'through and through' method.

Log cut using the 'through and through' method

Log cut using the 'quarter sawn' method described in the text

Equipment required for making sweet chestnut shakes

- Froe
- Mallet
- Bicycle inner tube
- Draw knife
- Side axe
- Shave horse.

Making shakes does require some fairly specialised tools. But by asking around, you may find someone who will lend you some. I certainly wouldn't have progressed with this project if I hadn't been able to borrow the shave horse, side axe and drawknife from a friend who works at the charity Dandelion Time.

Splitting the logs

The froe is a blunt blade, approximately 300mm long. It has a fitting at one end for a handle that allows it to be carefully positioned on the log. The careful positioning is critical and enables you to repeatedly strike the log in exactly the same place each time (important for tough sections of log) and to accurately cut the log in accordance with the quarter sawing diagram.

The mallet is almost a 'disposable' item. It should be made from a shock-resistant timber such as ash, which was also used for the froe handle. The mallet is simply created by cutting a ring around the perimeter of a log (about 150mm in diameter) and chopping away the timber to create a handle. The size of the mallet is an important element in how easy you will find it to split logs. The first mallet I created was too small and light. I had to use a lot of energy to get the mallet head going fast enough when I hit the log to split it. I also found that after a relatively short period of time, the handle broke. My next attempt at the mallet was much more robust. I also found that I needed to use much less force when hitting the froe, as the weight of the mallet head did most of the work.

▲ Froe, mallet and bike inner tube used for splitting the logs.

▼ Shave horse, drawknife and side axe in use for finishing the shakes.

▼ Comparison of traditional woodworking mallet and home-made wood splitting mallet.

Before splitting the log, take a moment to assess it. How straight is the grain? Are there any branches or potential irregularities in the wood? In addition, you may see a small crack in the end of the log (known as a 'heart split') – this will give you a clue as to where to place your first cut.

Before you start to split the log, stretch a rubber cycle inner tube around the outside. This will hold the log together after each split and makes it easy to keep a track of which cut you are on. The stretch in the inner tube allows you to

◀ Splitting a log with mallet, froe and inner tube.

▲ The first cut is the hardest, splitting the log in two.

rotate the blade of the froe to make sure that the split goes all the way down to the bottom.

The log is split sequentially, firstly in half, then into quarters and eventually into 16 pieces of pie. Each section of pie yields two shakes and one small triangle of waste wood. At least that is the theory.

In practice, the grain in the wood isn't straight. There will be knots in the wood that you can't do anything about, and also your skill (mine, certainly) in handling a froe and mallet may leave a little bit to be desired. However, at the end of splitting your first log you should end up with a decent pile of split timber, a good number of which have the potential to be good shakes.

Progress with the drawknife and side axe

The drawknife and side axe are used to remove the rough edges of the raw shakes and make them into components

◀ The log is then quartered.

▼ The log is finally split into sixteenths. In the bottom right quadrant, you can see where I have started to split each sixteenth into two shakes and a smaller triangle of waste wood.

▲ Pile of shakes immediately after removing the inner tube.

▶ Example of a hidden internal knot that makes a section of this log unusable.

▲ Using the drawknife to finish the top and bottom surfaces of the shake.

▶ Using the side axe to clean up the long thin edges.

that can be used to create a durable waterproof roof. The main part of the work is making the top and bottom and the sides straight and parallel.

The tools that are used for this shaping are the drawknife paired with the shave horse, and the side axe paired with the chopping block.

After sorting all the potential shakes into a single pile and leaving them near the shave horse, I found my best work arrangement was to sit on the sawhorse and alternate between using the side axe and drawknife until I had achieved a result I was happy with.

SHAVE HORSE

The shave horse is a very useful speed clamp and seat combined. The work item is clamped in the jaws of the shave horse by pushing with your feet. The strength of the clamp depends on the design of the horse (in this case about 3 to 1) so the pushing power of your legs is significantly magnified. The clamp can accommodate a good wide range of material thicknesses too.

With the prospective shake clamped in the jaws of the shave horse, the top and bottom of the shake can be made parallel. Sometimes the prospective shake is wedge-shaped and significant material needs to be removed. Other common situations are large ridges that would stop the shake sitting flat on the roof, or perhaps a bit of twist in the shake that requires excess material to be removed from opposing corners.

The end game of this stage is to have a shake that is approximately 15mm thick but may not, at this stage, have parallel edges.

SIDE AXE AND CHOPPING BLOCK

The side axe was used primarily for bulk material removal and making the edges parallel.

The side axe was useful for thinning shakes that were too thick to use but too thin to split further using the froe.

Once I had made the shake the correct thickness, I found that the edge closest to the heart of the tree was often a bit irregular and needed to be trimmed so that it was parallel with the grain. The edge closest to the outside of the tree would still have a couple of growth rings worth of non-durable sapwood left on. This small section of sapwood would be removed – the final result should be a lovely shake about 15mm thick and with all the opposing sides parallel.

Stacking of the shakes takes place in 'squares'. This means that with 450mm logs and using a three cover pattern for the roof, each square covers an area of roof 150 x 450mm (0.07 m²) which divided into the area of your roof will give you a rough idea of the number of squares that you will need to split to cover the roof. Allow a few over for the ridge and hip tiles too.

▶ 'Squares' of finished shakes in the background with logs, yet to be split, in the foreground.

6. Making the door and latch

Most sheds will use a simple ledged and braced door. Trying to make the door simpler by omitting the braces will only lead to problems in the future, as the door will sag and none of the door furniture will line up. Making the door more complex by adding a frame will greatly add to the quality of the door and its resistance to sagging and warping. However, this does come at a cost of greater time and complexity of fabrication. For the purposes of this project, we decided to stick with a well-made ledged and braced door.

The basic boards

To give you a full picture, we will start from the basic boards straight from the sawmill. It would definitely save you time to buy ready-cut boards with a tongue-and-groove profile, but would it be as much fun?

The boards that we used were 20mm-thick waney edge boards, which are almost a waste product from the sawmill that we bought them from. The first cut they make when creating a timber beam takes off the outer sapwood. This second cut then takes the next layer of timber off to get the beam to a uniform size. Sawmills often sell these boards as cladding timber for sheds. The outside edge of the board is the irregular outline of the tree trunk. Many people like this style of timber for cladding sheds, but for this project we wanted to cut the waney edge (and the sapwood) off the board and use the plank for creating a simple board and batten door.

Pictured are some of the waney edge boards that we bought straight from the sawmill. The boards as bought are

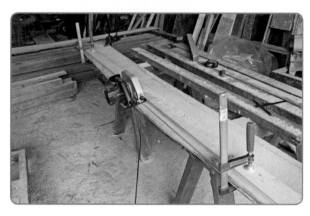

▲ Board clamped to bench and cutting off the waney edge.

often 'wet' and will need time to gently air dry (allow approx. one year per inch of thickness). To keep the boards relatively straight, stack them with timber spacers every 300–400mm and keep a weight on top while they dry out.

CUTTING THE BOARDS

Cutting the boards to width would normally be done on a table saw. For a small number of boards such as this, it is slightly more time-consuming – but relatively straightforward – to use a standard handheld circular saw. Use a straight floorboard as a straight edge for the first cut and then make use of the width guide, which is part of the saw's add-ons, to cut the opposite side.

When cutting the board you will need to use your own skill and judgement to cut off the sapwood while maximising

▼ Laying out and assessing the waney edge boards.

▲ Laying out the boards for the door.

the useful width of the board. It is also really helpful to inspect the timber and see what features you want to cut out or include. We definitely wanted to cut off the end checks and splits, but there were some interesting knot features that were good to include. The main priority, however, was to maximise the width of boards achieved.

ARRANGING THE BOARDS
Once you have cut the boards to width, the next step is to decide on the width and height of your door. The dimensions of the door for this shed were 600 x 1750mm. I cut the boards to length and laid them out to work out what I thought was the best arrangement.

When arranging the boards, it is important to take into account the orientation of the growth rings. Due to the nature of the boards, the outside of the board will expand and shrink at a different rate to the inside, leading to an effect known as 'cupping'. This can be mitigated by fixing the heartwood on the outside so that the screws/fixings clamp the board to the batten, keeping it as straight as possible.

ADDING THE BATTENS AND BRACES
Once you have the arrangement for your boards, it's time to arrange the battens and braces on the back. We used three boards across the back. The boards keep the face of the door straight and provide a connection between each of the boards.

The direction of the braces is important. Timber swells and contracts perpendicular to the grain but varies little dimensionally along the grain. So, having the braces sloping up from the bottom and middle hinge puts the brace into

▲ Close-up view of end grain. The board nearest the camera has the heartwood facing to the outside. The board next to it is placed incorrectly with the heartwood facing inward, and will be flipped over to minimise 'cupping'.

compression. This means that the weight of the door is trying to close the joint all the time and push the brace into the housing. If the brace was the other way up then the weight of the door would be trying to open the joint, which, given enough time along with wet and dry cycles, would

---

Commercial shed doors

When you take a look at doors on commercial sheds, you often see that they have one brace sloping up and one sloping downwards. I believe that this is to hedge their bets and so that they are guaranteed that at least one brace will be effective, whichever way up the door is hung.

▲ Laying out the ledgers and braces on the back of the door.

▼ Cutting in the braces with a chisel and mallet.

▼ Close-up of brace and fixings. Note that holes for screws are pre-drilled and countersunk.

happen. Then the door would no longer be square and start to sag.

Once you have decided on the arrangement for the ledges and the braces, mark these on the boards and cut out the housings. Using a chisel and mallet is the easiest way to do this.

A final touch for the ledges and braces is to plane (or use a router) to add a small chamfer to each of the exposed edges. This increases the visual appeal of the elements and also reduces the possibility of splinters and splitting of the edges.

Assembling the door

The door can now be fixed together. Use clamps to pull the boards together and also to hold the ledges and braces in position while you fix them in place. The traditional method of fixing the battens to the door was to nail from the 'front' of the door through the board and ledger. The end of the nail was then 'clenched', which means bashing the end of the nail over so that it couldn't be removed. With the advent of modern fixings, we chose to secure the battens and braces from the back of the door with screws, thereby giving the front of the door a less cluttered look.

Remember to use stainless-steel screws when working with sweet chestnut or oak. The natural tannins within the wood, which are responsible for the timber's durability, are acidic and promote corrosion in plain steel fixings. Moreover, sweet chestnut can be prone to splitting when relatively unseasoned, so pre-drilling and countersinking the screw holes reduces the possibility of this happening.

FIXING THE HINGES
The hinges are fixed next. Make sure you understand

▲ Fitting the hinges.

▲ Fitting the cover strips.

where the hinge pin sits in relation to the door opening so that you fit the hinge in the correct position. This will prevent problems further down the line when you come to hang the door.

ADDING THE COVER STRIPS
If you chose to make your door out of the more commonly available tongue-and-groove boarding then you can omit this step. Making a door from plain edge board means that gaps will appear between the boards, dependent on the season of the year and the moisture content of the door. The cover strips that we added are to keep out the worst of the

rain and wind. Though having a tongue-and-groove board or a loose tongue rebated between the boards is definitely an alternative solution.

We liked the appearance of the cover strips, especially after seeing something similar on ancient doors on a visit to our local pub.

TREATING THE DOOR
With the door complete, apply a couple of coats of linseed oil or teak oil. These treatments soak into the fabric of the timber and add to its natural durability. They also make it easier to recoat and maintain, as unlike paint they repel water and moisture does not get trapped behind them.

FINISHING TOUCHES
You will, of course, need some door furniture, a lock and/or a handle to secure the door. The best fittings at the moment are the 'long throw'-style locks, as used on the Bike Shed (see pages 30 and 127). These fittings use a Euro-style cylinder and have a 20mm square bolt with a metal housing that has sufficient tolerance to accommodate the sort of timber movement to be expected on a shed.

We chose to make a simple slide bolt out of timber for everyday opening and closing, with a more secure bolt for when the shed has contents that are to be left unattended.

◀ Completed door with coat of linseed oil.

▼ Simple timber slide bolt.

7. Making the siding

The siding that we chose for this project was Douglas fir feather edge board. Douglas fir is a medium durable timber. It is durable as a siding material but less durable than timbers such as oak or sweet chestnut, especially when in contact with the ground.

The profile of the timber that you choose for your siding will have a big impact on the appearance of your shed. Also, siding is one of the biggest items of initial and ongoing cost, so it is worth considering this item carefully.

The most common cladding material is untreated redwood or whitewood. Treated timber will last longer, although it is more expensive initially and tricky to deal with at the end of its life.

A top tip when installing siding on a shed such as this that you are building from scratch is to paint or treat all of the siding first before you install it. This way, you will ensure that all the critical faces that will get exposed to moisture are properly covered. End grain and the bottom edge of boards where drips of water can gather are critical places to coat properly.

For this project, and in the spirit of choosing the most interesting route, we opted to go for a version of the traditional Japanese method of wood preservation called 'Shou Sugi Ban'. This method was developed for use on cedar siding and is reputed to give wood additional fire resistance as well as exceptional durability. These are bold claims, but using a medium durable timber and coating it

▲ View of Douglas fir feather edge boards showing variation in the natural colour of the wood.

▼ Trialling different Shou Sugi Ban finishes.

with a timber oil should go quite some way to giving this siding a good long life. In addition, as you will see, it really shows off the timber grain, giving it a beautiful appearance.

Getting started
The principle of all cladding is that it is like fish scales and should naturally encourage water out and away from the internal fabric of the building. For cladding such as feather edge, this means that there is an overlap and relatively tight horizontal joint, each board held at intervals to keep it straight. At the corners, the boards need to butt up to a board or corner piece.

With those principles in mind, study the sketches of how the cladding works at the following locations:

- Corner
- Base of wall
- Top of wall
- The junction of two boards.

Make a list of the lengths of cladding that you will need to fit to your shed and cut them to length. Even if you don't use Shou Sugi Ban, and it does look great, I would recommend that you coat your siding before you fix it to the side of your shed.

Making Shou Sugi Ban siding
There are three main steps to making Shou Sugi Ban siding:

1 Char the timber
2 Brush off the charring
3 Coat with timber oil.

TIMBER CHARRING
The traditional method for charring the surface of the timber was to create a chimney of three planks and light a small fire at the base. Once it was judged that the surface was sufficiently burnt, the chimney was quickly broken apart and the fire put out.

It is a lot simpler to use a standard roofer's torch and a bottle of propane gas. To char the 15m² of feather edge for this project we used 8kg of propane. The key element of the roofer's torch is a regulator that can deliver a high flow of gas. The one that we used first was a low-flow one that maxed out at 0.5kg/hour and provided a weak yellow flame. The one that we ultimately used was a variable flow type that delivered a maximum flow of 8kg/hr and provided a powerful blue flame. **Follow the supplier's instructions for setting up the roofing torch, particularly with attention to specific safety instructions.**

With the torch connected up, open the tap on a low flow of gas and light the flame. Pressing the trigger should

▶ Detail of cladding at corner.

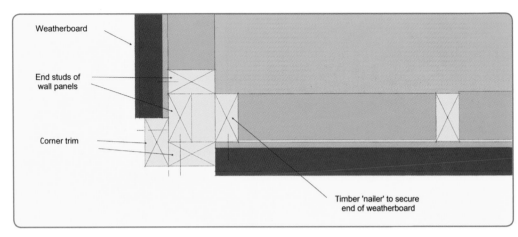

Weatherboard

End studs of wall panels

Corner trim

Timber 'nailer' to secure end of weatherboard

▶ Detail of cladding at base of wall.

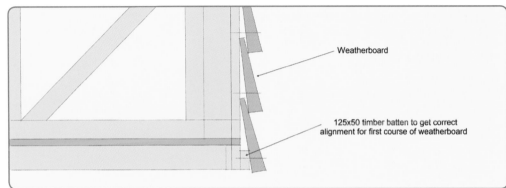

Weatherboard

125x50 timber batten to get correct alignment for first course of weatherboard

▶ Detail at top of wall.

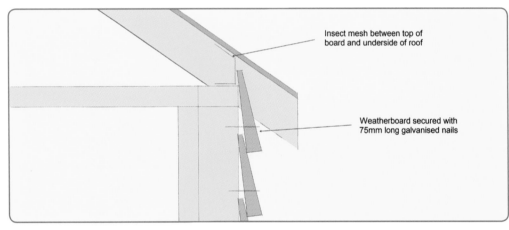

Insect mesh between top of board and underside of roof

Weatherboard secured with 75mm long galvanised nails

▶ Detail of cladding at junction of two boards.

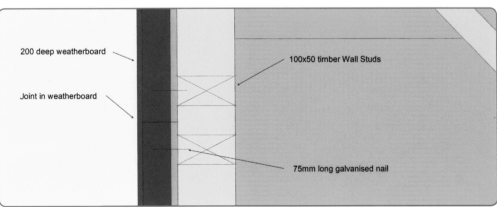

200 deep weatherboard

Joint in weatherboard

100x50 timber Wall Studs

75mm long galvanised nail

▲ Laying out the timber for charring.

◄ Starting to char a small section of timber.

change the flame from orange (low-ish temperature) to blue (high temperature). Experiment with passing the flame over the timber to get a feel for how to scorch it. You are aiming for much more than the slight singeing shown in the first photograph. You really know that you have got the right level of char when the surface of the timber has the appearance of 'crocodile skin'.

A top tip for arranging the timbers is to put them in rows and start from the bottom of the row working up, as in the picture. This means that you are pre-heating and charring the bottom of the next row as you work up.

When laying out the timbers, make sure that you lay them with the thick end facing down and the heartwood facing up. The reason for this is that the thick end of the feather edge is the edge that will be exposed, so needs charring properly. Also, as explained more fully in the door-making section (see page 91), timber tends to 'cup' as moisture content varies and it dries out. Having the heartwood facing outwards tends to minimise the impact of this.

BRUSHING OFF THE CHAR

To brush off the charcoal, use a wire brush. Our observation is that it is the softer timber that chars the most. So, as you brush off the burnt wood, you end up exposing the raised grain of the timber. Using the wire brush removes the structure of the charcoal, then use a soft brush or compressed air to remove any loose particles that are still on the plank.

COATING WITH TIMBER OIL

The traditional oil for protecting timber is linseed oil. Manufacturers have attempted to improve on this traditional method, firstly by introducing boiled linseed oil and then other additives. The main improvements are drying times and how deeply the oil soaks into the wood.

For this project we ordered some boiled linseed, but the supplier sent us some teak oil by mistake. We used it anyway. For the first coat, adding perhaps 20% of white spirit will help the oil to penetrate the wood and seal it. The second coat will go on a lot quicker. Apply a third coat if you think the timber still looks 'thirsty'.

The oil takes about 24 hours to dry and once it has done so, you can brush against the timber without it leaving dirty stains on your skin or clothes.

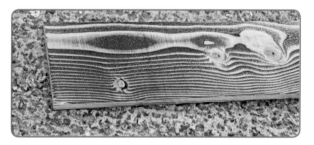

▲ Lightly charred timber.

▼ Timber fully charred and ready to be brushed.

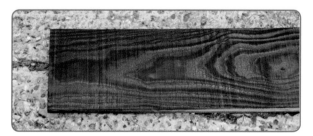

◄ Using a wire brush to remove loose char.

▼ Applying timber oil to small sections of cladding for use around the door.

8. Making the windows

▲ Using a chisel to loosen the first of the glazing beads.

▼ A screwdriver is then used to lever the glazing bead out.

▼ Window frame with first pane removed, showing removal tools and removed glazing beads.

▲ uPVC window with double-glazed panes ready to be removed.

As part of the theme of using recycled materials for this shed, we chose to use window panes that we recovered from some uPVC windows that were being removed as part of a house renovation.

Removing the glass

Removing the glass from the uPVC was fairly straightforward, as the pictures show. The double-glazed unit is held within the frame by PVC 'glazing beads'. The glazing beads are easily removed using a chisel and/or a screwdriver, along with a mallet. We found it easiest to use a chisel and mallet to initially prise the glazing bead out of its housing, then insert a screwdriver into the gap for a bit of extra purchase and leverage. Once you have the first bead out, the remaining sides are a lot easier, as there is a free end to push the screwdriver into.

With the glazing beads removed, the double-glazed unit can simply be lifted out and put to one side. Measure the exact size of the glazing pane and also the thickness – you will need to measure these dimensions exactly to make the window frames.

Making the window frames

The window frames for this shed are fairly simple affairs. Making windows for houses or sheds can be as simple or as complex as you feel necessary. Timber-framed house

◀ Double-glazed unit with 3 x 2 frame with housing cut.

windows are excellent for sheds, but these ones will still be robust and weatherproof.

We used a section of treated 3 x 2in timber for the frame. Using the window dimensions measured earlier, and a groove depth of 15mm, we calculated the lengths of window frame material that we needed and cut them to length. Using a router fitted on a router table, we routed a 15mm-deep groove in each internal side of the frame. For the short (horizontal) sides of the frame, the groove ran the full length of the member. For the longer (vertical) sides of the frame, the grooves were 'stopped', i.e. they didn't run the full length of the frame and we used a chisel and mallet to square up the ends of the grooves.

After a trial fit to make sure that the timber frame fitted around the double-glazed unit, we then used the pocket hole jig to make joints at each of the four corners of the window frames.

We stopped further detailing of the unit at this point, but it would be possible to add a drip groove along the bottom edge or to make a frame, so that the window would be opening rather than a fixed pane such as this.

◀ The frame with pocket hole screws holding the frame elements together.

Case study: Chris Routledge

I built my garden office in 2003, partly to free up space in the spare bedroom, and partly because, as a freelancer working from home, I needed a reason to get dressed and go out of the house at the start of the working day. With hindsight, it may also have had something to do with the death of my grandad the year before. He was a joiner by trade, and I remember the protective calm feeling when the door of his workshop shed was pulled shut, and the smell of sawdust and wood, hot from the circular saw. I think, deep down, I wanted something similar for myself, only with books and internet access.

The office was the first thing I had built from wood since the hopeless dovetail joints I made in the school workshop 20-odd years earlier, and I built everything from scratch and by hand; the only power tool I used was a circular saw to cut plywood for the roof and floor. I had to learn how to make a door, window frames and rafters for the roof. Accurate sawing was always my biggest challenge, more so because it was all by hand, and I was keen to minimise the amount of cutting. One unexpected side-effect from using hand tools was that my hands went up an entire work glove size during the build, and to

further boost the morale of a soft-handed writer, the local timber yard started giving me a trade discount.

Surprisingly little went wrong with the build, though I remember miscalculating the number of plywood sheets I'd need for the roof. Fortunately, I was able to make up the shortfall with offcuts, so if I had bought that extra sheet, a lot of it would have gone to waste. Since building the office I've added a bike shed extension on the side, and built a playhouse for my daughter, with a green roof. They have made me more confident about tackling carpentry jobs around the house, though they haven't made me get round to doing them any sooner.

As for the office, it is distinctly overbuilt for a garden shed, made with 3 x 2 timbers, roofing felt behind the tongue-and-groove cladding, and proper guttering to carry water away. I wish I'd been more generous with insulation, but it's easy to heat nevertheless, and 15 years on it is still a comfortable, warm, dry place to work, even in the depths of a Lancashire winter. This would be my advice to anyone self-building a workroom or office shed where you are going to be spending a lot of time: think of it as a small building, or a room in your house, and build it accordingly.

9. Installing sweet chestnut shakes

Traditionally, roofs were covered in materials that were available in the local area. So in the north of England slate and stone were used, while in areas such as Norfolk and Devon, thatched roofs were common. As transport links and industrial processes have improved, we have a wide range of roofing materials that are durable and easy to fix.

We mentioned earlier our concerns about using bitumen roofing felt for sheds (see page 42). Most of the felt that is sold is not durable and needs replacing every five years or so. As well as the recurring cost of the material, there is also the cost of your labour to replace the roofing. There is also the damage that occurs to the fabric of the shed and its contents in the period between the shed first starting to leak and you spotting the leak and getting around to repairing it.

Sweet chestnut shakes aren't the cheapest or easiest method of roofing a shed (that is EPDM, in our opinion) but they do offer a unique finish and character to your project.

Adding a membrane

The starting point for installing the roofing was to fit a belt and braces to this design. A waterproof breathable membrane is used beneath most tiled roofs. This membrane stops any drips of moisture that make it through the three

What's the difference between 'shingles' and 'shakes'?

Shingles are traditionally sawn timber roof tiles. Cedar shingles are generally sawn and have a smooth, regular appearance. Bitumen roof shingles are an extension of this, being smooth and of a regular size and shape.

Shakes, by comparison, are made by splitting the raw timber and so they are much thicker and more irregular in appearance.

cover system of overlapping tiles and then feeds the drips out to the eaves. The breathable aspect of the membrane means that any humidity from within the shed can migrate to the outside without building up and causing problems with condensation.

The membrane that we used had a detailed specification

▼ Breathable membrane installed on shed roof.

▲ Short, galvanised 'clout head' nails used for fixing the membrane.

▲ Battens screwed in place.

that showed the laps in our area of the country to be 100mm on the bottom and 150mm on the sides. We didn't use tape for the joints but did use extra-large head 20mm long galvanised nails to fix the membrane to the rafters.

Fixing the battens

The next step was to fit the battens. The shakes that we made were a minimum of 450mm long, so to give the full three cover, we needed to install the battens at intervals of 150mm. Measuring down the slope, you will need to determine the length of the slope and the number of intervals. For this

project, the battens needed to go right to the hip rafter. The 19 x 38mm battens that we used were relatively thin – this meant that although generally we didn't pre-drill the screw holes, when we were near an end or installing short lengths of batten we pre-drilled the holes to prevent the timber splitting.

Finally, to get the first row of shakes lying properly on the roof, we fixed an extra batten on the first row. This lifted the bottom edge of the first row of shakes (only two-thirds length) up so that it lay parallel with the next full length row that were laid on top of it.

Fixing the shakes

▲ The partially battened roof. Note the double layer of battens on the bottom row.

◀ Fully battened roof with bottom row of two-thirds length shakes in place.

▲ Shakes at the bottom of the roof.

▲ Close-up view of shakes at eaves.

50mm-long stainless-steel ring shank nails were used to fix the shakes. If you use plain steel nails for fixing sweet chestnut, you can expect problems with staining of the timber and corrosion of the nail due to a reaction between the steel and the natural acids in the wood.

A single nail was used to fix each shake and this was on the left side of the shake on the middle row of battens (see pictures). As the installation progressed, additional nails would pass through each row so adding to the security of each shake.

The first row of shakes was only two-thirds the standard length to get the roofing pattern started. This was nailed on the second batten up.

For the second and subsequent rows, the shakes are supported by three battens and nailed on the central batten. To minimise the possibility of the shakes splitting, fixing holes of 3mm diameter were pre-drilled to accommodate the 2.65mm-diameter nails.

The method of overlapping the tiles on straight sections of roof can be seen in the picture.

The hips and ridge were tricky parts of the project to install shakes. To ensure that these areas were fully waterproof, a 'soaker' tile cut from 2,000-gauge polythene was used to cover the joint at each course of shakes. The polythene was fully covered by the shakes and so didn't impact on the visual appearance. Polythene is not stable to UV exposure for long periods of time, as it loses its flexibility. So the polythene being covered by shakes was a double benefit of constructing the roof this way. The joint in the shakes was waterproof using this method, but to improve the appearance and make sure the polythene was fully protected from UV a series of 'bonnet' tiles was made using pocket hole screws (we told you that this jig was useful!) and fixed to the roof over each of the seams.

Finishing touches

The finishing touches to the roof were to add guttering to the perimeter. Collecting the roof water from a shed is one method that you can use to prolong the life of any shed. Sheds tend to degrade from the bottom up. The 'splashback' from rainwater hitting the ground near the shed base makes the bottom of the

cladding damp for extended periods during wet winters. Damp timber degrades much more quickly, so anything that you can do to keep it dry will make your shed last longer.

The other touch to add is an insect mesh around the junction between the roof and the walls. Having a barrier such as this will keep out insects, birds and bats, so that you are left to your own devices in your shed without unwanted visits from curious critters.

▼ Cutting 'soaker' tiles from heavy-duty PVC.

▼ Soaker tiles under and overlapping shakes on hips and ridge.

10. Installing the siding

We looked at what you will need at critical sections of the shed when we went through the list for the shed siding, prior to treating the timber (see page 94).

Installing the corner membrane and corner blocks

The first part of siding installation is to install the corner membrane and cover pieces where you have any planned joints in the siding. Then install the corner blocks, as this sets the frame for the limits of the siding boards.

Installing the batten

You will need to install a length of batten along the bottom of the wall to 'kick out' the bottom of the first board. This simulates the way that subsequent boards are angled by the board below.

Fixing the boards

Fixings for this siding don't need to be stainless steel (not oak or sweet chestnut) but it is recommended that galvanised nails are used to prevent rust staining as the structure weathers. To prevent splitting of the boards, especially close to their ends, we would recommend that you pre-drill holes prior to nailing.

The boards are fixed to the side of the building with one nail each time the board intersects with a wall stud location. The nail is located just above the top of the board below. This means that the bottom of each board is fixed to the structure by a nail while the top of the board is clamped to the structure by the nail holding the bottom of the board above.

When fixing boards, we made our first fixing near the

▲ Corner membrane was used at panel joints.

▼ Additional batten required at the bottom of the wall to 'kick out' the lower edge of the first row of weatherboard.

▼ Installing and levelling a board.

▲ Using the spirit level to check for level.

▲ Pre-drill holes to minimise potential of boards to split.

▼ The fixing from inside. The board above clamps the top of the board below, holding it in place.

centre of the length of the board and then made sure that the board was level (using the spirit level) and in alignment with the rest of the shed before drilling and fixing the next nail. With the board fixed by two nails, the rest of the nails along the length of the board could then be fixed.

With the first board fixed, you will have determined by how much you want to overlap the boards, and so measure and mark on at least one stud where you intend to locate the top of each subsequent board.

Continue working up the wall, fixing the boards in place and stepping back every now and again to check that everything still 'looks right'. As you get within a couple of

▼ Cutting out the notches to accommodate the rafters.

▲ Trial fitting the notched board.

► The notched board fixed in place after it has been charred and oiled.

rows of the top, it is time to mark out the gaps that you need in the top board and to cut out the gaps to accommodate the rafters.

We have included a few pictures to show how fixing of the siding works at items which are less standard than just a straight run.

The building is now getting close to being weathertight! Let's move on to installing the doors and windows.

▼ Use double wall studs and membrane where a joint in the boards occurs.

▼ The cladding around the doors and windows.

11. Installing the doors and windows

▲ Trial-fit of doors and windows in the workshop.

▲ The door, roughly in place.

The door and windows were trial-fitted to the openings before we moved the shed out of the workshop. We fitted the door once we had taken the shed out of the workshop to a location in the yard.

Fitting the door
We fitted the door first. We had already fitted the hinges as part of the door-making process. The door hinges were to be fixed to the 4 x 2 door lining that was fixed to the shed frame and also formed an edge for the siding to butt up against.

The shed door was relatively heavy. After roughly positioning the door in the frame, we used wedges (cut on a slope of 1:6) to adjust the door for height and level. Using a hammer to tap the wedges in made aligning the door fairly straightforward.

With the door in position, the hinges could be fixed into place using the screws supplied with the hinges.

The door 'shoot bolt' was fixed to the middle batten of the door and a recess marked on the door lining to accommodate the bolt. The recess was cut with a mallet and chisel, as was the hole through the door to accommodate the dowel and door handle.

Installing the windows
The windows were installed into the rough opening in the framework. The timber window frame was secured to the shed using screws through pre-drilled holes driven at 45 degrees into the shed framework. A sill made from cedar was used below the window and angled using timber wedges. The gaps around the window were covered in strips of Douglas fir siding that had been charred and treated in the same way as the rest of the shed.

▼ Using wedges to lift and align the door.

▼ Hinges screwed into position.

12. Moving the shed

The easiest way to move a shed is to dismantle it into its component panels. However, sometimes it is better to move a shed in one piece. That was the case for this shed. I built the shed in a barn workshop and then needed to move the shed out into the yard to its final position. I decided not to completely assemble the shed in the barn to save a little on weight.

The strategy was to move the shed 'Egyptian style', using rollers. The first step was to use a hydraulic bottle jack to lift up each end of the shed in turn to remove the screw jacks from each corner of the shed.

The barn floor was of rough compacted chalk, so we used some scaffold boards to create a smoother running surface until we got the shed out of the barn and onto the smoother concrete surface of the farmyard. We had to make sure that at least two rollers were under the shed at any one time.

With the shed lowered onto rollers, it moved forward surprisingly easily. Possibly the trickiest thing to do was to 'steer' the shed. This was achieved using a scaffold pole to lever the front of the shed into the required direction.

▶ The rollers were 100mm diameter, 2.4m long wooden fence posts.

▼ The shed is just out of the barn. Using a scaffold pole to help steer the shed around a 90-degree bend.

▲ Scaffold boards were screwed to the underside of the shed and also used for the running surface in the barn.

▲ As poles were removed from the back they were carried round to the front of the shed.

▲ Approaching the final location of the shed.

◄ The shed in place requiring final levelling.

► Jacking the shed up again to insert the screw jacks and adjusting for level.

The general direction of travel was downhill, but even moving up a slight incline would have been possible. With one person concentrating on the steering, the other removed rollers from the back as they became free and brought them round to the front.

The shed was eventually in its final resting place about 50m from where its construction had started. The jacking process was reversed to lift the front then the back of the shed up so that the screw jacks could be inserted into the base frame and then adjusted for level.

► Shed in final position with siding, doors and windows fixed.

SHED 3: BIKE SHED

1. Overview

▲ The bike shed.

The bike shed is the smallest of the sheds in this book. For the purposes of planning, any shed built forward of the front elevation of a dwelling needs planning permission. However, some local authorities may cast a blind eye to small bike sheds such as this, as the height is such that they are below the fence line and they encourage active travel, keeping yet another car off the streets, but it always wise to check.

This type of shed is also ideally suited to the storage of garden equipment, such as barbecues, deck chairs and small tools. The small plan size and the lifting lid means that any item can be easily reached from the front of the shed. The shed has been designed with security and ease of access in mind:

▼ General view of bike shed concept.

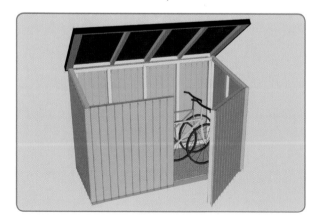

Security
- Both of the front doors have spring-loaded bolts that slot into the floor
- The top of the doors are secured to the roof
- The screws for all of the hinges are inaccessible when the doors are closed
- A Euro-cylinder lock has a discreet brass cover plate and is protected by the front roof overhang.

Ease of access
- Two gas struts help with lifting of the lid, as well as making the lid safe when it is in the lifted position
- The lock is of the 'long throw' gate type. This allows for movement of the door and is very secure, with a 20mm square steel bolt between the two doors
- The two front bolts are easily lifted by pulling internal chains to release the doors.

Although this is the smallest of the sheds in the book, it contains many features that could be used on larger sheds.

▶ Bike shed lock.

Starting at the base

The shed has four adjustable feet. This type of shed is suited to being located on a hard surface such as a patio or driveway. So having these feet with 50mm of adjustment allows you to get the base of the shed level on a surface that has a slight slope. In addition to the levelling benefit, having the shed lifted up in the air means that none of the timber is in contact with the ground and air can flow beneath the shed. This means that the base timbers will stay drier, leading to a longer life for the shed.

The floor of the shed is not heavily loaded and so a 12mm formply has been used. This has water-resistant glue and so is resistant to delamination. The floor of the shed will not be constantly wet but will get damp occasionally when wet bikes are put in the shed or in extremes of driven rain.

Doors

The doors utilise extra-long 'broad butt hinges' – the benefit of these is that the extra-wide hinge plates push the hinge pin beyond the edge of the door. This means that even with 20mm-thick cladding on the face of the door, it will still open outwards without the cladding catching. Also, the screws securing the hinges are always concealed, thus improving security.

The doors are framed and braced using pocket hole screws to make the joints in the door frame members. The exterior is clad in sweet chestnut timber, which is naturally very durable.

Roof

The roof is hinged with strap hinges (fixings concealed on the inside) and waterproofed with an EPDM rubber covering. This membrane is glued to the roof deck rather than using nails and being clamped around the perimeter. Both these factors mean that the roof will have a long life without leaking.

A 'drip edge' is fixed to the front edge of the roof. This encourages roof water to form drips and fall off, rather than flowing back up under the roof due to capillary action or in gusts of wind.

The roof is locked to the doors in the 'closed' position. When the lock is released, two gas struts help to lift the roof and hold it open while you access the contents of the shed.

Frame

The frame is constructed from a combination of 2 x 2 and 3 x 2 treated softwood. The pressure treatment protects the timber

▲ The shed, with gas struts raising the roof.

▶ Close-up of gas struts.

from prolonged moisture. The members are connected with pocket hole screws. This method of connecting timber is stronger than the traditional method of screwing together timber, and in addition the joint has a neat appearance, with the screws being concealed within the timber itself.

The framework is constructed as a series of panels. The panels are connected with heavy-duty 'coach screws'. The benefit of using coach screws is that the hex head is unaffected by corrosion and so the shed can be easily dismantled if it needs to be moved to a new location.

Cladding

The outside of the shed is clad with sweet chestnut timber. The cladding is fixed in strips, which allow some airflow between them. This means that moisture from damp bikes or contents can evaporate and escape. Using a hardwood means that the outside of the shed is very durable, while an initial coating of decking oil increases this further. Sweet chestnut has a similar expected lifespan as oak.

Inside the shed

The shed has the capacity for 'onion-like' security features. Once you get into the shed, there is the facility to install a steel rail along the back to which you can bolt your bike so that any potential thief who gets into the shed still has to spend time and make further noise to remove the steel chain securing the bike to the rail.

Also, internal shelves could be added to provide space to store accessories such as helmet, pump, tools and puncture repair kit.

2. Framing joints

The starting point for building the bike shed is to construct the frame. The two commonly used methods for joining timbers for a shed such as this are using ring shank nails or screws to 'skew-nail' the timbers together, as in the image shown. For this, three nails are driven into the timber at an angle: two from one side and one from the opposing side. This combination of three fixings locks the end of the timber in position.

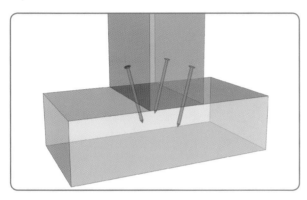

▲ View of skew nailed joint.

The pocket hole kit

The basic pocket hole kit comprises:

■ **Angled drill jig**
■ **Stepped drill bit with collar to control depth of drill**
■ **Long driving bit**
■ **Pocket hole screws**
■ **Clamp**
■ **Drill.**

▼ Pocket hole kit.

For this project, the timber size was relatively small and at some points there were several members coming together at different angles at the same point, making 'skew-nailing' impractical. So we opted to use an increasingly popular method of joining timber, called the 'pocket hole joint'. This method involves drilling angled holes into one of the members and using flat head 'pocket hole' screws to connect the members.

The advantages of using pocket hole joints are:

■ Neat appearance
■ More strength than nailed joint
■ Easy to move and reposition member
■ Easy to install angled members
■ Accuracy of installation.

The downsides are that some special equipment is required and the cost per fixing is higher than for using standard ring shank nails. However, once you have a pocket hole jig, you'll find all sorts of repair and construction projects become easier. Go on, you know you need one!

How to create a pocket hole joint

The main piece of equipment is the jig that directs the drill into the end of the timber at the correct angle and height. This jig has an integral clamp and base. Other brands of jig comprise only the angled part, for getting the correct

▲ Close-up view of pocket hole jig.

hole angle, and are clamped into place with a quick-release bar clamp.

To get the right proportions of the screw in each piece of timber and to get a good clamping force, the jig needs to be set at the right distance from the end of the timber. In this type of jig, the distance is set by raising and lowering the angled part of the assembly.

The piece of timber is then clamped in the jig. There are three

▼ Pocket hole jig guide and depth adjuster.

▲ Timber clamped in pocket hole jig.

▲ The joint clamped in position, and using a drill/driver to install the screws.

different hole options to choose from. The trick is to get the holes as far apart as possible, while also allowing a sensible distance to the edge of the timber. For the 3 x 2 members, we chose holes A and C; for the 2 x 2 members we chose A and B. The main factor was to get the screws not too close to the edge of the timber but as far apart as possible.

Before drilling the joints, make sure that the collar on the drill (adjusted with an Allen key) is set at the right distance from the end of the drill. Each system has a slightly different method for this, based on the thicknesses of timber being connected.

Finally, drill the pocket holes in the location required.

▲ Drilling the holes for the pocket hole joint.

The resulting joint will look something like this (see below).

To secure the two members together, a method of controlling the alignment of the members is needed. For the joint shown in the image, the joint was held at 90 degrees

▼ Pocket hole joint with screws.

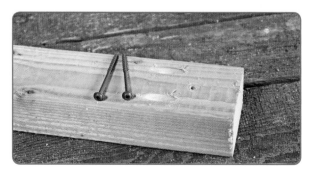

and prevented from slipping by using a purpose-made clamp, but a standard quick-release bar clamp would do equally well.

When tightening the pocket hole screw with a drill/driver, make sure to set the torque to a relatively low setting. Too high a setting can mean the driver will strip the thread through the receiving piece of wood.

▲ The joint with a number of pieces of timber converging at one point.

Using this method of joining timbers, neat and strong joints can be created quickly and easily.

What do I do if I accidentally strip the thread of a pocket hole joint?

Stripping the thread of a pocket hole screw can happen if you have the torque setting on your drill/driver set too high. This is not a disaster and the joint can be repaired fairly easily.

1 Firstly, remove the screw.
2 Dip a wooden toothpick in wood glue so that it is coated with glue for a length the same depth as the pocket hole.
3 Insert the toothpick into the pocket hole and snap it off.
4 Align the joint and replace the pocket hole screws, this time using a much lower torque setting.
5 The additional timber glued in the hole enables the screw to cut a new thread and make the joint strong again.

3. Constructing the base and walls

The construction of the cycle shed comprises a series of panels that, once made, are then bolted together. The sequence of panels as we built them were base first, then sides and finally the rear wall.

Constructing the base

The arrangement of the base is as shown in the sketch on the right. Working from a detailed design means that you should have a firm idea in your head of what to build – this makes it much easier to order the correct quantities of materials from the builders' merchant and minimises repeat journeys and delivery costs.

The base is constructed of 3 x 2 treated timbers and has four adjustable feet for easy levelling. This means that it can be assembled on an existing slightly sloping drive, patio or hardstanding. Alternatively, a pad base is easily made from four paving slabs supported on compacted stone.

The timbers are firstly cut to length and joined using pocket hole joints.

FIT THE FEET

The adjustable feet for the base comprise a 12mm threaded rod with a plastic foot and a pronged tee nut that will accept a 12mm diameter metric thread. The plastic foot has an adjustable joint to take up any small irregularities in the foundation.

The adjustable foot is fitted to the base by drilling a 12mm-diameter hole through the bearer and then counter-boring this hole with a 14mm-diameter drill to a depth of about 15mm (the depth of the pronged tee nut). The pronged tee nut is placed over the hole and then gently tapped in with a rubber mallet. The threaded part of the foot

▼ The adjustable shed foot and pronged tee nut.

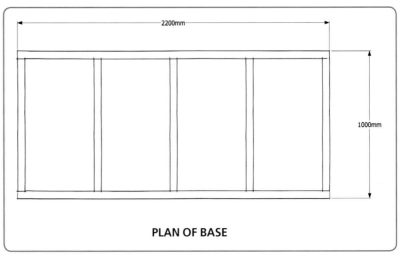

PLAN OF BASE

2200mm

1000mm

can then be screwed into the tee nut. The foot needs to project into the support timber by at least 50mm to make it stable.

► The adjustable shed foot in place.

▼ The shed floor, supported by an adjustable foot.

FIT THE FLOOR

The frame is then checked for squareness by measuring across the corners. Adjustments are made by tapping the corner on the longer measurement until the diagonal dimensions are equal.

The decking for the bike shed floor is made from 12mm formply. This material, like most sheet goods, comes in 2.4 x 1.2m (8 x 4ft) sheets. This type of plywood uses waterproof glue and has one 'good' side where holes, splits and irregularities have been filled/smoothed, and one rough side.

The floor for the shed is smaller than the size of a single sheet of ply. The plywood is cut to size using a handheld

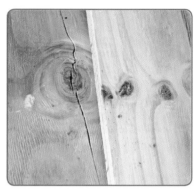

◀ Two full sheets of formply.

▶ Close-up of formply, showing the contrast between the smooth and rough faces.

circular saw with some bar clamps to secure a straight edge of timber to act as a guide.

The rough side is used face down with the smooth side exposed to view. The plywood is fixed to the squared frame using 30mm-long screws at 300mm centres, the length of the screw being approximately 2.5 times the thickness of the sheet material that it is securing.

Making the side panels

The sides of the shed are formed from 2 x 2 timber, cut to length and connected with pocket hole screws. The sides have a cladding of 22mm-thick sweet chestnut timber slats of 50–70mm width. For this shed, the timber cladding is fixed with a spacing of about 7mm between slats. The gap between the slats allows airflow through it. This means that any bikes that are put away wet can dry out. The small spacing between the slats and the roof overhangs will only let in very limited amounts of wind-driven rain, so the shed contents are protected from the elements.

For this shed, we cut the slats from waney edge boards, following the instructions overleaf. To save time and/or money,

pre-machined softwood boards could be used. Softwood isn't as strong or as durable as sweet chestnut, but with the shed lifted off the ground, the base of the shed is well protected from damp and the all-round roof overhang protects the sides well from rain. So this would be a good time and cost-saving option.

▼ The side panel frames.

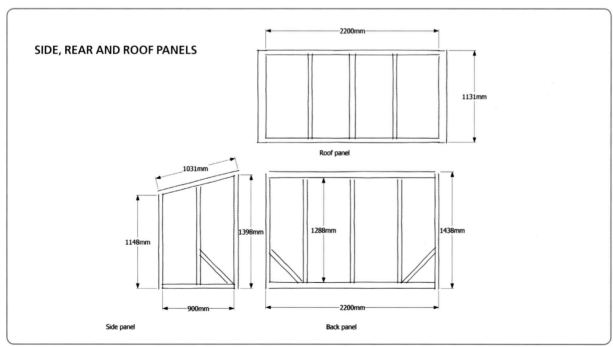

SIDE, REAR AND ROOF PANELS

2200mm

1131mm

Roof panel

1031mm

1148mm

1398mm

900mm

Side panel

1288mm

1438mm

2200mm

Back panel

Cutting strips from waney edge boards

Sawmills often discard the top cut when creating timber beams from logs. These boards are often of mixed quality, with either one straight and one waney edge or two waney edges. Depending on the species, these boards can be useful. Sweet chestnut is especially attractive, grown locally (so not many 'woodmiles'), and contains a very high percentage of heartwood vs. sapwood. It is only the outer four to five growth rings of sweet chestnut that contain sapwood, which are vulnerable to rot and insect damage.

▲ Waney edge boards.

Waney edge boards are often used without the edges removed as horizontal cladding on sheds and barns. For this application, we cut off one of the wiggly edges and then cut as many strips as possible of between 50 and 70mm width to create 'battens' to use as vertical cladding on the bike shed.

Cutting the boards is a time-consuming exercise in comparison to buying the boards pre-cut. However, it can be enjoyable, as the overall cost of buying hardwood cladding in this way is lower than buying the pre-prepared boards – and it is a good reminder of how timber makes the journey from tree to finished product.

The tools for cutting the timber are very few. We used:

- Four quick-release clamps
- A handheld circular saw
- A timber straight edge, longer than the waney edge board
- A pair of sawhorses or bench to support the timber off the ground.

1 Secure the boards onto the bench/ sawhorse using two of the clamps.

2 Find the best line for the edge of the batten. This is a balance between removing the softer sapwood and maximising the amount of heartwood that remains. Use the two remaining clamps to fix a straight edge on to the board (we used an old floorboard) then cut off the waney edge using the handheld circular saw.

▲ Securing the waney edge board to the bench.

▼ Cutting a strip using a straight edge to guide the saw.

3 Cutting the second and subsequent battens is a bit more straightforward, as the straight edge you have just cut can be used as a guide.

4 When cutting these thin strips, remember to use your spare hand to support the section of timber that you are cutting off.

▼ Subsequent cuts are made easier by using the saw's built-in guide.

Fixing the side panels

Whether you use pre-machined boards or cut your own siding boards, you will need to fix them and cut them to shape on the side of the shed.

If you use a timber such as oak or sweet chestnut, make sure that you use stainless-steel ring shank nails. The acidity of these timbers, which is related to their natural durability, will react with moisture to corrode normal steel nails, as well as creating unsightly rust stains.

TREATING THE TIMBER

Another tip is to pre-paint or treat the timber that you use before you nail it in place. It is much easier to paint all surfaces of the cladding before it is fixed to the shed. Lay the cladding out on some timbers or sawhorses to keep it off the ground.

We treated the timber for this

▲ Treating the timber prior to fitting it to the shed frame.

project with decking oil to give it extra waterproofing and UV resistance. Sweet chestnut is a naturally durable timber with similar durability to oak. Over time, most timber left to naturally weather will turn a greyish colour, dependent on its exposure to the sun and rain. Many people like this pattern of natural weathering, but if it's not for you then there are some excellent coloured wood stains that will give you solid blocks of colour (see page 31).

FIXING THE SLATS AND BATTENS

The slats need to have one end cut to the same slope as the roof of the shed, 14 degrees. The slats were then roughly placed to check that sufficient had been cut. We used plastic

▼ Shed with variable weathering pattern. The wood that is more exposed to the sun and rain at the bottom of the shed is much greyer than the wood sheltered by the eaves.

spacers to get an even spacing and the battens parallel. The first of the battens was fixed in line with the back edge of the shed and then we worked towards the front. After the halfway point, make a check to ensure that you keep a track of any 'creep' in the batten coverage. You may need to adjust the spacing to ensure that the last batten lines up with the edge of the panel.

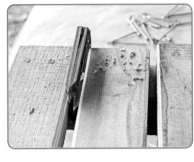

▲ Using plastic spacers to get the right distance between slats.

▲ Second nails in pre-drilled holes prior to being hammered home.

With all of the battens fixed with one nail, complete the nailing of the battens so that each has two nails per intersection with the frame. Pre-drilling the battens and making sure that the nails are not parallel will prevent splitting of the wood and give the nails extra holding power.

TRIMMING THE BOTTOM OF THE PANEL

The final step was to trim the bottom of the panel so that the base of the battens were the same length. We made it

▲ The completed side panels.

so that each of the battens projected 50mm past the bottom of the frame. This largely protects the base from water running down the side of the shed.

Creating the frame for the back of the shed

It was anticipated that the shed would be located up against a wall or hedge and not be as visible or accessible as the sides, so the cladding for this was chosen as pre-cut Douglas fir feather edge boards. This timber is a naturally durable softwood so doesn't require any treatment apart from the precautionary coating of decking oil.

4. Making the doors

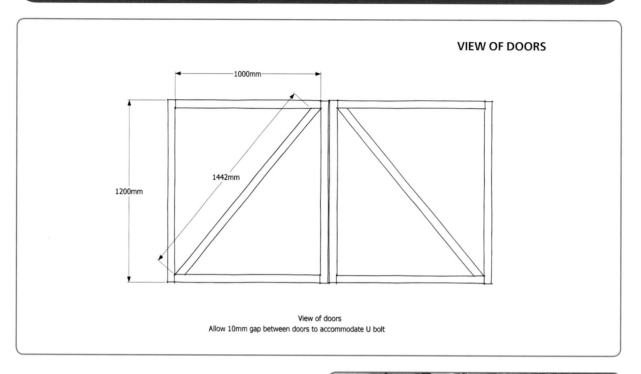

VIEW OF DOORS

1000mm

1442mm

1200mm

View of doors
Allow 10mm gap between doors to accommodate U bolt

The doors are a key part of this shed design. Of course, they hinge open to allow access to the interior of the shed. But the way they lock into the frame at the bottom and the roof *and* with each other at the top makes getting into the shed (when you have the key) easy and convenient.

Making the doors

The basic door framework is formed using 2 x 2 timbers using pocket hole joints. The diagonal brace is essential to keep the door square and stop it sagging in use.

Making the angled cuts clean and precise is easy using a mitre saw. The saw can be rotated about the horizontal axis to the exact angle required for the ends of the brace.

Slats for the door are cut to length and additional

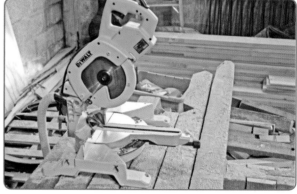

▲ Using the mitre saw for the cuts.

▼ View of door frame with brace.

▼ The protractor on the mitre saw enables precise angled cuts.

protection in the form of decking oil is applied before fixing the slats. As mentioned earlier, the slats are made of sweet chestnut timber, so stainless-steel ring shank nails are essential to avoid unsightly rust stains.

While the slats are drying, the hinges and provision for the door lock can be fitted.

The door hinges used are 'broad butt' hinges, similar to normal door hinges but with plates that are extra-wide. This means that the hinge pin is pushed forward of the door post so that when the 20mm cladding is fixed, the door can still open 180 degrees without clashing with the cladding on the door post. As the shed is designed to be permeable to air, for ventilation, it is not

▲ 'Broad butt' hinge.

necessary to create a recess in the door or the door post to accommodate the depth of the hinge.

SECURING THE DOORS

The door is secured to the adjoining door with a 'long throw lock'. These are a relatively recent innovation, developed primarily for gates, but they work really well for securing sheds of all types. A secure Euro-cylinder lock with a brass plate is visible from the front. The mechanism is located on the back of the door; turning the key through 360 degrees moves an 18 x 18mm stainless-steel bar 65mm horizontally.

The bar passes through a steel keep, which is bolted to the adjoining door. The keep has dimensions of 24 x 35mm, which give a bit of tolerance for external timber doors/gates that have a tendency to expand and contract with variations in the outside temperature and humidity. In addition to securing one door to the other, the doors are designed to have a gap of 10mm between them. This gap is to accommodate a 'U bolt', which is fixed to the roof. When the roof is pulled down, the U bolt fits into this gap. When the lock is turned, the bolt fixes the doors to each other and the roof.

The lock is fixed through a purpose-made timber insert fitted between the door brace and the outer edge of the door. The insert, which is cut from 4 x 2 timber, is secured in place by pocket hole screws. The screws are located to allow for a 25mm hole to be drilled to fit the lock mechanism. The hole is located far enough down the door so that the keep can be bolted to the door, but not so far down that the U bolt fixed to the roof is too long.

▲▶ Timber insert to allow fitting of the long throw lock.

FIXING OF THE BOTTOM OF THE DOORS

When the oil has dried on the slats they can be fixed in place. It is recommended that holes for the nails are pre-drilled

through the slats. Hardwoods such as sweet chestnut and oak are prone to splitting if they are not pre-drilled. Two nails are used at each intersection with the door timber and a 3mm hole is drilled for the 2.65mm-diameter nail.

We used plastic spacers to get an even spacing between the slats. An initial spacing of 7mm was used. Remember to re-measure the distance from the edge of the slats to the end of the door when you get past halfway, so that you can make minor adjustments to the spacing if necessary and to ensure the last slat ends at the end of the door.

Two slats on the door containing the body of the lock were cut short and the top ends chamfered to make space for the lock.

When all the slats had been nailed to the door frame, the doors were put to one side and a trial assembly of the shed started.

TRIAL ASSEMBLY

The shed is designed so that it can be taken apart and reassembled. This is useful if you are moving house or if your needs change and you want to move the shed to a different part of your garden.

A trial assembly enables you to check that all the individually made components fit and also to install parts that occur at the interface between two panels. Examples of this are the top braces, the bottom door bolts and the roof frame.

The trial assembly starts with getting the base level. Use a spirit level and adjust the feet screwed into the tee nuts in the shed base. This is good practice for the final assembly. First of all, get the base level on each short side. Then the two feet on one end can be adjusted, the same amount up or down, so that the base is level along its length.

The walls are attached by placing an end panel in position so that it lines up with the end and front of the base. Then

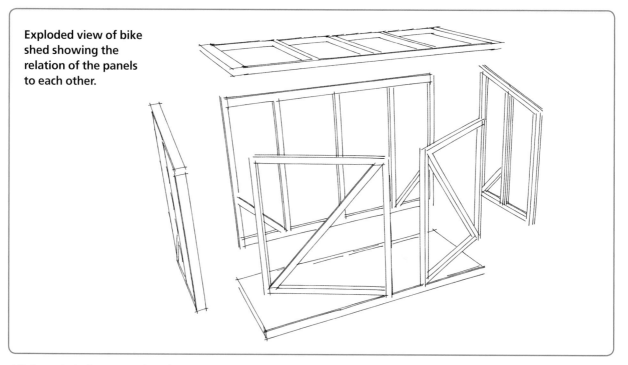

Exploded view of bike shed showing the relation of the panels to each other.

drill through the bottom timber of the wall, through the plywood floor and into the timber that forms the edge of the base. Use a 10mm drill bit for this. Then change the drill bit for a 12mm drill bit and re-drill the hole, this time only passing through the bottom timber of the shed wall.

The wall is fixed to the base using 12mm hex-head coach screws. The screw passes through the bottom of the shed

▼ The partially assembled shed. The base is level and the side panel is fitted. The rear panel is about to be installed.

wall and you will need to use a socket and ratchet to tighten the bolt and cut into the timber base. Having the larger hole above means that the coach screw achieves a clamping action. Two screws are needed to fix the end walls to the base and three to fix the rear wall.

Hex-head bolts are used as they are easier to undo when you need to dismantle the shed and move it to another location.

The side walls are connected to the rear wall with two coach screws. The holes are formed in a similar way as those for the base, although an additional counterbore is required with a 25mm spade drill bit. This is so that the head of the screw can be tightened so that it sits below the surface of the timber. The end timber slat is screwed in place rather than nailed (using stainless screws) so that it can be removed, to give access to the bolts fixing the side panel to the back when the shed is dismantled.

With the sides and rear wall in place, the doors can be installed. The process for hanging the doors is to pack the

▼ Close-up view of panel to base fixing.

▲ Packing up the outer edge of the doors while fitting the hinges.

◀ Broad butt hinges were used for the doors.

▲ General view of braces to stop 'side wall flex'.

▶ Close-up view of mitred end of brace.

door up on the outer edge so that the top of the packers are level with the shed floor. Then an additional 5mm spacer is added to both the top of the timber packers and the shed floor. The door is then lifted in to position and the hinges screwed to the door post. We found it easiest to first of all put one screw in each hinge to hold the door in place. Then add the rest of the screws, so that all of the holes are filled. Having an extra person on hand to support the door and pass tools was very useful at this stage.

With the doors hung, you will notice that the weight of the door tends to flex the side walls. Installing the diagonal top braces counteracts this and enables the adjustment of the doors. Cut two lengths of timber as shown. Be careful to get these right as the two pieces are similar but 'handed' mirror images of each other. One end of the brace has a simple angle with the saw rotated only about the vertical axis. The opposite end has what is known as a compound joint. This means that the saw is rotated about both the horizontal and vertical axis.

The accurately cut braces are secured in position with pocket hole screws. Once again, it can be tricky to get the holes in the right place due to the braces being handed. A useful tip for cutting the braces correctly is to hold the brace in position and mark approximately where the holes should be using a pencil. Then when it comes to placing the pocket hole jig this becomes a double check that you have the holes in the right place.

Once you have cut the braces, get into the shed and close the doors. There should be a 10mm gap between the ends of the doors (the space for the U bolt from the roof) and use a 5mm spacer beneath the end of the door. Fix the braces in place using your drill/driver.

The next items to fit are the spring-loaded bolts to the

bottom of the doors. With the door in the closed position, screw the bolt to the vertical outside edge of the door. Mark in pencil on the shed floor the position of the bolt in the closed position, then get the metal keep that comes with the door bolt and place it over where the bolt will sit. You will need to cut a square hole in the plywood floor to accommodate the bolt and the lip where the edge of the metal keep is folded down. The plywood is easily cut using a 15mm chisel and mallet. Screw the keep into position and you are ready to move on to the next stage.

▶ Tools and setting out for the spring-loaded bolts.

▼ Spring-loaded bolts installed.

5. Constructing the roof

The roof of the bike shed is a key element. It keeps the contents dry, it is an important part of keeping the bike shed secure, and the way it is hinged and uses gas struts to lift it means that the contents are easily accessible (for those that have a key!).

An important part of the bike shed design is that the roof slopes forward. The shed is designed to be located against a wall or fence, so if the roof sloped backwards the water would run into a badly ventilated gap and before long the back of the shed would rot. Having the water drain to the front of the shed means that once it drips off the roof, it can drain away or evaporate.

Having the roof slope forwards creates a slight problem for access into the front of the shed, as it becomes quite low. This problem is overcome by using gas struts to lift the roof. Gas struts are an underused secret in the shed world. They act like a damped spring and make it easy to lift a heavy item such as this shed roof, which weighs almost 30kg, with one hand.

When the shed roof is open, access to all the contents is easy and it is simple to find and remove whatever you are looking for in the shed.

Building and installation

The roof is made of a combination of 3 x 2 and 4 x 2 timbers, using pocket hole joints as described earlier. The reason for using the larger 4 x 2 timbers is to achieve a side overhang for waterproofing purposes and also to give enough space to install the roof hinges.

We made the mistake of installing the hinges after we had fixed the OSB roof panel. The roof panel adds a lot of weight to the roof, so we recommend that you install the hinges before fitting the OSB board.

To fit the hinges, firstly secure the strap hinges to the top of the side wall. Make sure that the hinge pin slightly overhangs the end of the frame. Having this overhang means that the roof won't clash with the back panel when it is lifted into the open position.

You will then need some assistance to hold the roof panel in place as you fit the first screw in the hinge at each side. Once you have the first screw in place, the position of the roof is set, so double check that it opens smoothly and isn't going to clash with the frame or cladding. Your assistant will then need to hold the roof frame in the open position until you have all of the screws in place.

With the roof frame secured, you can cut the roof panel to size. We used 12mm OSB 3 for the roofing. Using the correct grade of OSB is important – only OSB 3 is made with waterproof resins that will resist getting damp occasionally, although this will be a rare occurrence with the EPDM roof membrane.

The roof panel is fixed to the frame with 35mm-long screws (no need for stainless here) at 400mm centres on each of the struts.

▲ Roof frame in position.

▲ Installing the 12mm-thick roof panel.

► Learn from our mistake and install the hinges before you install the roof panel!

▼ The roof propped open while installing the hinges.

▲ Roof membrane laid out on roof deck.

INSTALLING THE WATERPROOF MEMBRANE

With the roof panel in place, it is time to install the waterproof membrane. This membrane is made out of EPDM (see page 40 for its suitability for domestic shed use). The first step is to spread it out on the roof, making sure that the edges are parallel to the edge of the roof and that there is an equal overhang (at least 150mm) all the way round.

The glue for the roof is applied using a paint roller. The glue (make sure you get this when you order the roof membrane) is poured into the paint tray. For this roof, we applied the glue in two stages. To start, we folded back the roof covering, exposing half of the roof deck, and applied the glue to the first stage. We then carefully folded the membrane over the glued area, trying to avoid creating any

◀ Roof adhesive in tray with roller.

▼ Apply adhesive to one half of the roof deck and then the other.

air bubbles. With the membrane in contact with the roof deck, we used a soft broom and our hands to remove wrinkles and air pockets and make sure that the membrane was in contact with the OSB deck.

We then repeated the process for the other half of the roof.

FIXING THE ROOF TRIM

With the membrane glued in place, the roof trim can be fixed. The roof trim serves the purpose of clamping the edges of the membrane in place and protecting the edge of the roof from small impacts where it is most vulnerable. The trim also gives a nice 'finished' appearance to the roof edges.

Before fixing the roof trim, the corners of the membrane are folded, as shown in the picture. Folding the membrane in this way gets the excess membrane out of the way and also means water can't collect in the fold. Each fold is secured in place with a single nail through the membrane into the side of the roof frame.

Sweet chestnut strips were used for the trim to the sides and back of the roof. These will get wet occasionally from the rain, but won't have significant water flowing over them. We used

▲ Close-up view of fold at corner of roof membrane.

stainless-steel screws for securing the trim and countersunk each of the holes. When fitting countersunk screws into hardwood such as sweet chestnut you will need to pre-drill the hole and also use a separate bit for the countersinking. If you don't have a purpose-made countersunk bit for your drill, you can use a 10mm or 12mm wood drill and just use the very end of the drill to create the recess for the screw head.

Adjoining pieces of trim use a simple overlap joint at the corner. Don't try to get too fancy by using a mitred joint at this point. Over time, it will likely warp and not look as good as the less sophisticated, but more robust detail shown in the picture.

▶ Timber trim at top edge of roof.

▲ Use tin snips to cut the metal trim.

▲ Close-up view of metal trim forming drip edge at front of roof.

The front edge of the roof is trimmed using a piece of standard plastic coated metal angle trim bought from the roofing supplier. The trim (only 1mm thick) is cut to length using a pair of tin snips. Don't be tempted to use an angle grinder. The heat from the grinding wheel will melt the plastic coating on the trim and the finish to the cut metal is far neater using tin snips.

The long edge of the trim points downwards and the angle is secured with self-drilling roofing screws, which were supplied with the angle. To ease installation, we used a centre punch to create a small dimple to locate the end of

the screw at each of the four fixing locations. These roofing screws use Torx head bits to give the driver some extra 'bite' and also have a rubber washer beneath the head to give a seal between the metal angle and the roof membrane.

The roof construction is now largely complete. The only remaining items are to add the gas struts for lifting the roof, and the locking U bolt on the front edge. These could have been added at this point, but we thought it best to wait until the shed was installed in its permanent location.

▼ The shed on completion of trial assembly.

6. The final assembly

Building sheds panel by panel and fitting them together over time allows for the type of extended build that most DIY shed builders will experience. If possible, it is good to work under some form of shelter where you are protected from the rain and sun. This also means you can leave the timber out and not have to put it away each time you finish work, and that you can utilise small parcels of time like fitting in an hour before you leave for work or when you get back, so as not to leave the whole project to the weekend.

Fitting in small jobs allows you to press the project forward and also allows some time for your brain to think about and solve problems that you are having with the build and to arrive at creative solutions. And, of course, doing a trial assembly and final build allows you to iron out small problems on your second attempt…. So, let's get started with the final assembly of the bike shed.

The location of the bike shed was on a brick paved driveway with the back of the shed up against a hedge. Just to remind you that sheds are not usually permitted forward of the front elevation of a dwelling, so the siting was a bit controversial, but I understand that although potentially contravening planning, some councils may cast a blind eye to this type of installation.

3 The back wall was installed and bolted to the base and the end wall.

4 The end wall has a cover strip externally that covers the bolts that secure the panels together. The opposite end panel was installed and cover strip fixed in the same way.

1 The first part of the installation was to level the base. This passed with flying colours; the ground was sloping but the adjustment on the feet coped with room to spare.

2 The first end wall was installed and bolted down to the base using the coach screws into the holes drilled in the trial assembly.

5 An assistant was needed to help lift the roof panel on. Then our lovely assistant lifted the lid, enabling us to fix the end screw into the hinges. With a screw in each hinge, the lid was then opened further and the remaining screws were inserted.

▲ Top fixing (left) and bottom fixing (right) of gas strut.

Installing the gas struts

The gas struts bring this shed to life. A bit of care is required when installing them. Each of the gas struts can apply a maximum force of 500N (50kg), which is more than most people can compress by hand, so don't give it a try.

With a component that involves some relatively large forces, it is important to make the end anchorages secure. We used some 3mm-thick stainless-steel angles and fixed each of these to the side wall and roof with eight 50mm long 4mm screws. The gas strut has a ball joint with a threaded end that can be bolted to the side of the angle, as shown.

The gas strut used was 500mm long when open and 300mm closed, with a force rating of 500N. Gas struts are a fairly common piece of hardware, largely due to their use for lifting car boot lids. Adjusting the angle of the roof or position of the anchorage points from those shown will give you different results as to how easy or difficult it is to raise the lid. Don't worry – a small amount of experimentation will get you the end result that you need.

The gas strut is fitted with the roof open. When fitting gas struts, ensure that they are installed with the piston (the thin end) pointing downwards. This is important for the long-term durability of the seals, as the oil in the gas spring will flow downwards and keep the seals lubricated in the closed position.

The ball joint is secured to the gas strut using a small

6 The lid was fairly heavy and needed to be propped open with a length of timber so that work could progress on installing the doors. The doors were installed in the same way as previously, by using packers and spacers.

7 With the doors in position, the top braces were installed to ensure that the doors swung freely.

We used a clamp and an extendable timber to help us to get the doors working correctly, with a 10mm gap between the ends of the doors to cater for the securing bolt.

▼ A gas strut in place.

spring clip. This little bit of hardware lives up to its name and can spring off, so keep a watchful eye when removing or replacing it.

The top end of the strut is fitted on the ball joint and the securing clip is positioned. The lid is then raised or lowered so that the bottom ball joint can be connected and clipped in place. The struts always work in pairs to avoid twisting the roof, so install the strut at the opposite end in the same way.

The moment of truth is when you try to close the lid. There should be a bit of initial resistance and then the roof should just pull down as you compress the gas inside the strut. After you pass a certain point, you will feel the lid close under its own weight.

Then, just for the experience, open the lid. You should just need one hand to start the lid moving – after you have lifted the first few inches, the gas struts will take over and do the heavy lifting for you. The roof will continue raising until it is in the open position.

Installing the U bolt and bracket to secure the roof

The roof is secured to the door bolt by using a U bolt.

The installation process starts with finding a suitable U bolt. The one that we used was a 10mm-diameter bolt with 48mm between the two ends of the bolt, and it was 98mm long. We then got a small folded metal channel made to secure the bolt to the middle roof timber.

We drilled the roof timber to accommodate the sections of the U bolt projecting back into the roof timber. You will need to work out the dimensions for this item to suit your own situation as locks and bolt dimensions might not be exactly as we have used in this project.

The combined U bolt and channel fitting was then screwed to the roof timber. Great care was taken to get the length of U bolt and distance from the end of the channel to match the location of the door bolt.

One final wrinkle to get the door to lock easily – first time, every time – is to screw a wooden 'stop' on to the central wooden spar to give the doors something solid to close against. This means that as you close the doors, they end up

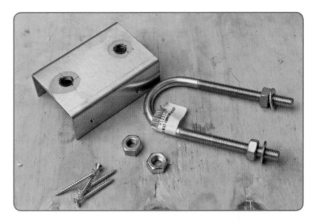

▲ Metal fitting for fixing U bolt to roof timber.

▶ How the metal channel and U bolt connect together.

pushing against something that is fixed to ensure that the door bolt aligns exactly with the hole in the U bolt. Getting the locking system to work is a bit fiddly but is well worth it, and you will be pleased that you spent the time each time you open and close the gas-assisted roof.

▲ Drilled roof timber.

▼ U bolt and door bolt with one door open, showing how the two work together to secure the roof.

▼ Fitting screwed to roof timber.

SHED 4:
ECO SHED

1. Overview

This shed is the largest of the builds covered in this book and also the one that was longest in the planning stage with the longest construction period. We are going to focus on three elements of the build:

■ Manufacturing the roundwood timber frame from scratch
■ Erecting the frame on site
■ Installing the roof, floor and solar panels.

Alister had wanted an outside family/party space for over ten years. With an interest in sustainability and minimising the impact of building work, he had been researching building methods for a good part of this time. Sustainability was at the core of this project.

The size of the shed was to be 3.5 x 8m and the aim was to provide a relatively airtight space that would be wind- and weathertight, but would not be insulated.

To minimise the construction impact, Alister's strategy was to:

■ **Source local construction materials where possible** – the structural frame was made using sweet chestnut poles grown in Sussex, the shed was to be clad in waney edge elm from trees under ten miles from the site
■ **Use responsibly sourced materials such as FSC timber when local timber was not available** – the timber joists, plywood and OSB for the floor and walls were sourced from a local builders' merchant
■ **Re-use and repurpose existing construction materials** – the foundations were built using crushed

For the full build...

We have included some details of installing the walls and floor. But for full details about the walls and floor, as well as the choice and installation of doors and windows, John has created a section on **secrets-of-shed-building.com** for you to find out more.

concrete and paving slabs from neighbours' building projects. The roofing tiles were reused from a house that had been recently demolished. All of these required some physical input from Alister but proved low-cost and low-carbon methods of construction

■ **Incorporate renewable power into the project by installing solar electric panels** – almost the whole of the south-facing roof slope was covered in solar panels. This provided enough power to recharge the batteries for a Nissan Leaf electric car and for Alister's electricity meter to occasionally go in reverse.

To achieve all of the above aims required a fair degree of planning and an extended construction period. Occasionally, construction would pause until materials for the next part of the project became available. Once construction started on site, the build took just under eight months.

Alister had the ability to mobilise large numbers of helpers – there were 15 people on site for raising the structural frame – and he also used his wide network of contacts to source materials that aren't available 'off the shelf'.

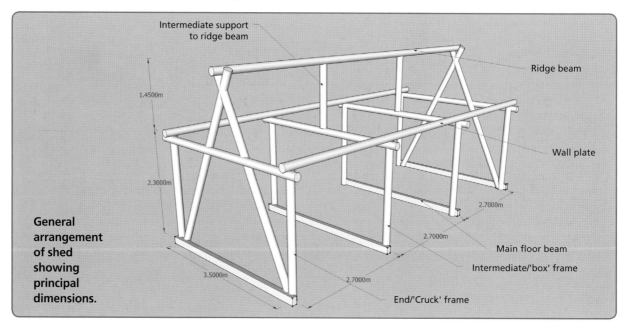

Intermediate support to ridge beam

1.4500m

2.3000m

3.5000m

2.7000m

2.7000m

2.7000m

Ridge beam

Wall plate

Main floor beam

Intermediate/'box' frame

End/'Cruck' frame

General arrangement of shed showing principal dimensions.

2. Constructing the frame

▲ Just a few of the timber framing tools used on the roundwood construction course.

For cutting
- Debarking spades
- Drawknives
- Rounding planes
- Side axe
- Cleaving froe
- Variety of chisels (standard framing chisels, as well as slick, gouge and corner chisels)
- Variety of specialised drills and augers.

For clamping
- Carpenters' trestles
- Shaving horses
- Ratchet straps
- Clamps
- Dogs
- Superjaws
- Framing pins.

For measuring
- Spirit levels
- Chalkline
- Carpenters' squares
- Log scribers
- Profile gauges.

The frame for the shed was built by Alister and others on a timber framing course run by Ben Law at his workshop at Prickly Nut Wood in West Sussex.

Ben first came to the public's attention when he was featured on television in *Grand Designs*. The construction of Ben's woodland house was one of the most popular episodes and the project was certainly one of presenter Kevin McCloud's favourites. In contrast to many of the projects in the series, it was delivered to programme and on budget.

Alongside managing his woodland, Ben runs courses teaching the skills of timber framing. A comprehensive description of the process of building using round timber is contained in Ben's book, *Roundwood Timber Framing*.

Tools and materials
WOODWORKING TOOLS
A number of fairly specialised woodworking tools are needed in the construction of a roundwood timber frame and the process of converting raw chestnut poles into a structural unit. This list above gives you an idea of the range of tools and equipment you will need.

MATERIALS
The raw material for the frame is coppiced sweet chestnut logs. This type of timber is used for the purpose due to:

- **Durability** – the timber has a high content of heartwood, which contains natural tannins, giving the majority of the log a durability similar to that of oak
- **Strength** – the timber has an allowable stress slightly less than oak but much higher than softwood construction timber
- **Eco-credentials** – the natural tannins in the wood mean that it needs no chemical preservative treatment. Also, the timber is grown by a method that is known as coppicing. The timber poles are cut off just above the stump level on a 15–30 year cycle, dependent upon the use. The timber then regrows from shoots at the stump level leaving the ground beneath undisturbed. This method of forestry is beneficial to biodiversity, as it results in a wider variety of different habitats for woodland creatures than standard clear felling methods.

▲ Raw logs and the first debarked pole with debarking spade.

▶ A drawknife is used to finish the bark removal.

PREPARING THE LOGS

The timber poles for the building are selected for construction on the basis of shape (straightness or curve), degree of taper, length and absence of branches. A greater degree of subjectivity and experience is required in the selection of appropriate logs in comparison to going along to the builders' merchant and buying sawn timber.

With the logs selected, the bark is removed. A debarking spade is used for removal of the majority of the bark and then a drawknife is used to give a finer finished surface.

With the logs debarked, they are transferred to the framing bed. This is a series of timbers set out to form a level frame. The height and spacing of the framing bed timbers provides a solid space to firmly hold the poles in position while they are being worked on. The spacing of the bed off the ground means that access to the frame can be gained from above and below. The poles are held in position on the bed using nylon webbing ratchet straps.

▲ The framing bed.

▼ First pole in position on framing bed.

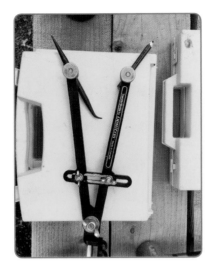

▶ The Veritas log scriber is used to transfer the profile of one log on to another.

▶▶ Concentration and practice is required to master the art of log scribing.

FORMING THE JOINTS

With the poles held firmly in position on the framing bed, joints can be marked out prior to cutting out the timber to form the joints.

The basic joints used to form this frame were:

- ◼ Mortice and tenon
- ◼ Cogged cruck
- ◼ Dovetailed notch.

▶ Pencil mark on log transcribed from shape of log below.

▶▶ Finishing cutting 'dovetailed notch' (butterpat) joint.

SECURING THE FRAMES TOGETHER

With the joints marked, cut and strapped tightly in place, the connections can then be drilled to receive the oak pegs that secure the frame members together. The oak pegs are made from seasoned, kiln-dried oak. The initial shaping of the pegs, from square to roughly cylindrical, is made using a drawknife on the shave horse. Final shaping is made using a rounding plane to make a peg of 1in diameter.

◀ Tie beam with 'butterpat' joints cut.

▼ Frame members cut to receive tie beam.

▲ Mortice on top of jowl post to receive longitudinal tie beam.

▲ Pre-rounded oak peg held in the 'Superjaws' with a rounding plane for finishing.

▲ Steel framing pin used to align frame joints during final adjustment of joints.

In addition to the frames, longitudinal members were needed to connect the frames and eaves at ridge level. These poles need to be long and straight with minimal taper. As they won't be exposed to the elements in the same way as the frame members, the same level of timber durability wasn't required. 8m long larch poles were used for this purpose with some small machining using a chainsaw to get the top and bottom surface parallel. Final cutting of the mortices was to take place on site when the frames were erected to meet final site tolerances.

During the week-long course that Alister attended, an end frame and an intermediate frame were completed by the eight course attendees. Two similar frames were completed on another course to finish the frame construction.

When the frames were completed at the end of the summer, they were put to one side in storage until the site was ready for the frame erection the following March. One factor that enables the prefabrication of sweet chestnut frames in this way is the minimal drying distortion that takes place in roundwood timber.

In contrast, in square sawn green oak structures, the frame must be erected fairly quickly following drilling of the

▼ Ben inspects a finished oak peg.

holes in the frame. The distortion of the frame then holds the oak pegs in place permanently. For the sweet chestnut frame, the round timber isn't cut and so the distortion doesn't happen. This leads to a slightly different pegging technique that is covered in the next section when the frame is erected.

◀ Long larch poles for use as eaves and ridge beams.

▼ Marking out poles for locations and adjustment at mortice locations.

3. Erecting the frame members

Before the frame members could be delivered, the site of the new shed needed to be cleared and the bases prepared. An old shed had occupied the site previously and this was dismantled.

Preparing the foundations

The new shed was to be supported on eight 'pad foundations', set out to match the base locations for the frame. These pads comprised a pit approximately 600mm square and dug to a depth of 600mm, where good firm ground was found. The pit was then filled with hardcore (builders' rubble) compacted by hand using a compaction plate in 100mm layers. The compaction plate was a 150mm square of cast metal on the end of a wooden pole. This was raised and dropped repeatedly to compact the hardcore into a dense, solid mass. The top of each of these pads was capped with a recycled concrete paving slab to support the feet of the frame.

Preparing the frame

With the foundations complete, the frame poles, which had been in storage since the previous summer, were delivered to site.

The poles had been marked during construction as to their

▼ The construction site after clearance of old shed.

▼ The pads almost complete.

▼ The top of a pad with marking to match pole.

◀ Frame poles after being offloaded at site.

▶ Steel alignment pins used for initial locating of frame joints.

▼ First two poles of the end A frame in position.

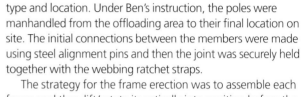

type and location. Under Ben's instruction, the poles were manhandled from the offloading area to their final location on site. The initial connections between the members were made using steel alignment pins and then the joint was securely held together with the webbing ratchet straps.

The strategy for the frame erection was to assemble each frame and then lift/rotate it vertically into position before the next frame was assembled. Each frame joint was temporarily connected before lifting using the alignment pins and ratchet straps. Once the frame had been erected, the pins were removed and seasoned oak pegs inserted and secured before the ratchet straps could be released.

Lifting the frames was heavy and potentially dangerous work. Ben was in control of each lift and significant preparation was undertaken to ensure each lift went smoothly.

There were two key preparations for lifting the frame. The feet of the frame were secured against slippage by

◀ Ben demonstrating using alignment pins and ratchet straps.

◣ Frame joint with alignment pin and secured with ratchet strap.

▼ Section through 'cruck' frame.

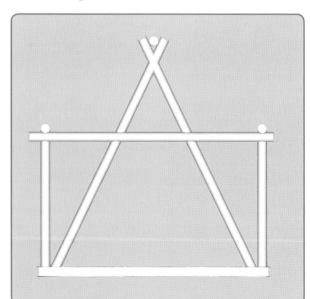

▲ The feet of the frame were painted with bitumen to give them additional damp resistance.

▲ TimberLok bolts and 4 x 2 timber to temporarily brace the frame once it was vertical.

driving a steel post with an eye welded to the top into the ground adjacent to each base. A rope was then attached, connecting the post to the base of the frame.

Secondly, the base of frame members in contact with footings was painted with black bitumen. The top of the pads were designed to be dry and shed water, and the sweet chestnut timber is very durable, even if in full ground contact. But the bitumen was there as an additional precaution to protect the end grain from 'wicking' up any dampness. Although the sweet chestnut is rot resistant, any timber will eventually succumb to decay if water is present, so this was a nice touch to protect the timber.

A supply of TimberLok bolts, milled 4 x 2 timber and torque drivers were on hand to brace the frame once it was in the vertical position.

Lifting the frame

Before the lift, Ben made sure that the team understood the sequence of work and that each member of the team understood their role.

▲ Ben briefing the team.

▼ The start of the lift.

▶ Frame lifted 45 degrees – no turning back now!

▼ Frame in vertical position.

◤ And relax! Frame vertical and temporary bracing in position to secure it.

SECURING THE OAK PEGS

With the frame vertical, the joints could now be made 'permanent'. The 1in-diameter oak pegs made during the course were produced.

The alignment pins were 20mm diameter, 5mm less than the holes in the frame. The permanent oak pegs are of the same diameter as the holes in the frame.

To secure the pegs in position, the end of the peg is

▼ 1in-diameter oak peg.

▼ Bucket of pre-made oak pegs.

▲ Cutting the wedges for securing the oak pegs.

▲ Ben driving the first oak peg into position.

▼ Cutting a split in the end of the peg.

▼ Driving the wedge into place.

sawn with a Japanese-style pull saw to give a narrow slot into which shallow taper wedges are driven to hold the pegs in place.

ASSEMBLING AND LIFTING THE OTHER FRAMES

The second of the frames was a 'box frame'. This was much lighter than the end 'cruck frame' and comprised two upright 'jowl posts', a horizontal tie member at eaves level and the floor beam. This frame was much lighter than the first but still a significant weight. The same technique was used

▶ Section through the intermediate 'box' frame.

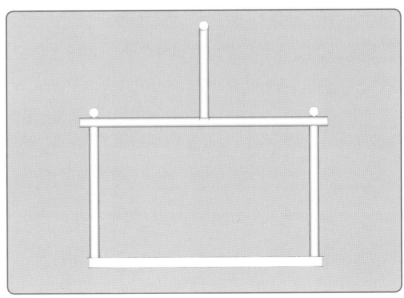

▲ Team in place before the second lift.

▲ Frame up at 45 degrees.

▲ Frame vertical.

▲ Bracing the second frame so that it could be left free standing.

◄ The first two frames erected and with temporary bracing complete.

▼ The excitement was just too great for some!

▲ The last of the four frames erected and braced.

▲ View from inside showing frames with floor beams spanning between pads.

for assembling and then rotating this frame from the horizontal to the vertical.

With each lift, the team became more practised in the lifting technique. Ben's experience made sure that safety was at the forefront and nothing was overlooked.

The assembly of the next two frames continued using the same techniques and methods as for the first two.

INSTALLING THE WALL PLATES AND BEAMS

With all four frames erected and temporarily braced, it was time to install the wall plates and ridge beam (see diagram on page 130). These horizontal members extend the whole length of the building. In the case of the wall plates, they connect onto the tenons at the top of the jowl posts, with site marked and cut mortices. The ridge beam sits in the V created by the two poles crossing on the cruck frame. Additional intermediate vertical supports are later added to support the ridge beam on the horizontal member of the box frame.

The eaves beams were made on the frame construction course. The key design element of this member is to remember that it tapers. Flat notches are cut at the locations where the jowl posts connect to the beam. The depth of the notches are arranged to take out the taper of the pole and result in the top surface of the round pole running

▲ Ben checking a few dimensions with the four frames in place to ensure that the eaves beams will fit snugly on the jowl posts.

◣ End view of frames before eaves and ridge beam were lifted into place.

▼ The tenon on top of jowl post.

▲ The wall plate with notches cut.

horizontally to give a common support level for the feet of the roof rafters.

As with the rest of this frame, the wall plate is not featherweight. Lifting a member of this length and weight into position was made easier by the many hands available and Ben's experience of manhandling heavy and unwieldy constructions.

Marking and cutting the mortices

When all three of the longitudinal members had been lifted into place, it was time to accurately mark and then cut the mortices that would ultimately hold the four frames together. To enable the marking of the joints, the wall plate was lifted into position on top of the tenons and the location of each joint was marked.

▲ Carrying the wall plate from the drop-off point to the structure gives the team an idea of the weight of the item.

◀ Lifting the far eaves beam into position.

◀ Lifting the ridge beam into position. Ladders were used to lift the end of the beam over the 'horns' of the crossed cruck members.

▲ Wall plate in position to enable marking of mortices.

▲ Close-up view of wall plate sitting on top of jowl post tenon prior to marking.

▲ Framing chisel used for cutting out mortices.

▶ Cutting out mortice in wall plate.

As there were plenty of volunteers on this project, each joint was cut by a different person. The mortice locations were marked in pencil and cutting was started with a framing chisel and mallet. Once the initial housing had been cut, assistance was provided by Ben, who cut out a significant part of the 'meat' in the mortice using a drill, making finishing the joint much quicker.

▼ Drilling out mortice.

▼ The drilled-out mortice.

Case study: Theo

I live on a boat and when my partner became pregnant we knew we would need somewhere for relatives to stay when they visited, as our boat was too small to accommodate them. Our mooring site has a lovely bit of communal land with it and I knew there was an abandoned shed up in the woods. The plan was to turn this in to an insulated summerhouse with a wood-burning stove, some simple built-in furniture and a sofa bed. The shed could be used by anyone who lived at the moorings and has become a focal point around and in which we hold parties, gatherings and meetings.

I think it's handy to start a project with a plan or a vision. We chose Van Gogh's painting, 'Bedroom in Arles' as the inspiration for how we wanted the shed to look when finished.

On closer inspection, the 3 x 3m shed had a completely rotten floor and sub-frame, a collapsed and rotten roof and the walls were decayed and wobbly – but apart from that it was fine.

It was satisfying finding the exact matching T&G cladding to replace all of the rotten boards, and surprisingly simple to clad downwards from the sound boards at the top of each wall. There was a noble feeling about the resurrection of this humble shed and we knew we were preserving this 1990s original, soft wood and OSB shed for future generations to enjoy. How much of the original shed is left is debatable, a bit like Trigger's broom….

One real stroke of luck we had was finding exactly 9m² of mahogany floorboards in the brambles next to the shed. They must have been removed from an old boat that had moored here before. It turned out to be exactly the right amount to refloor the shed, and the shed now benefits from a solid mahogany floor.

Once the roof was replaced with corrugated bitumen roof sheets, we were ready to insulate and clad the inside. I was given some glazed timber patio doors, which I resized to fit the opening. I like to think the doors are reminiscent of the windows in Van Gogh's painting.

If I were to do this again, I would probably beef up the roof structure, as the roof sheets sag a little where they overhang the edge of the shed. My tip for other shedbuilders would be to have some roofing slates handy to level the subframe with. They snap easily and are incredibly strong used in compression.

In my job as a carpenter, I have built all kinds of garden offices, treehouses and a tiny house on a hay trailer, among other things. It was interesting in rebuilding this shed to see how in mass-produced products they really push the boundaries in how small the structural timbers can be. The shed had no strength in its component parts and only stopped wobbling when the weight of the roof was on it. Not that I will be adopting this approach in my work anytime soon!

Arborhouse: arborhouse.co.uk

▲ View of the almost-completed frame the morning after the barn-raise. Fitting the support struts to the ridge beam. Note that the structure is still stabilised longitudinally by temporary bracing – this would only be finally removed once the walls were in place.

The details of this part of the construction have taken a fair chunk of description. However, in contrast to the fabrication of the frame, this part of the project was very quick. From completion of the foundations (hard work), the frame erection was completed in just over a day. The four frames including the wall plates and ridge beam were erected in one day with some additional work to install the supports to the ridge beam on to the box frame on the morning of day two.

With the frame erected, a huge part of the project was complete. However, there still remained significant sections to complete to make the shed watertight and weathertight for its intended purpose.

The next stage was to install the rafters and roof covering. Ben kindly delivered this pile of timbers to form the rafters and main floor beams.

▼ Timber to be used on the next stage: rafter installation.

4. Installing the roof

In contrast to the excitement of having 15 people on site, assembling and erecting the whole structural frame in just over a day, the roof construction was a much more sedate and painstaking process.

Installing the rafters

Continuing with the low-impact theme, the rafters for the shed were supplied by Ben. The rafters were made from 4in-diameter poles that had one face milled flat with a chainsaw. The top end of the rafter was then cut at a 45-degree angle to match that of the roof slope.

The challenge to fit these rafters of variable depth to a wall plate and ridge of varying height was to get the straight top surface of the rafters aligned, so that when it came time to fit the tiling battens onto the roof they would line through nicely, giving a smooth surface to the finished roof.

To achieve this level surface, notches were created in the ridge and wall plate, using a framing chisel and mallet, of a depth such that the rafters lined through.

To achieve the 'lining through', the end rafters were fixed first and string lines stretched between them. Rafters were installed at intermediate points along the string line to help with sag in the line. String lines were used at the top and bottom of the rafters – not much could be done if the rafters weren't straight at this point, apart from to select another straighter piece of timber. Thankfully, all of the rafters were pretty true.

Once a rafter had been lined up with the string line by creating a notch of a suitable size in both the ridge and wall plate, the rafter was secured in position. For a relatively short run of roof such as this, it was acceptable to secure the rafters with stainless-steel TimberLok bolts. Stainless steel

▲ Pile of rafter poles with one milled flat surface.

▶ Rafter held temporarily in position with TimberLok screws.

▼ String lines and cut ends of rafters at the ridge.

▼ String line fixed to rafter at one end of roof.

▲ View of the rafters with flat upper surface.

▲ About half of the rafters installed.

was used because we were fixing into the potentially corrosive sweet chestnut.

The rafter installation process continued until all the rafters were installed on both faces of the roof.

Working at height

Working at height was a weak point on this project – it made the roof installation slow and potentially dangerous. We would recommend if you undertake a project of this nature that you install a perimeter scaffold with a working platform at eaves level beneath the roof. It will make the installation of the roof much more 'comfortable' and speed the installation of rafters, roof membrane and tiles. Much time and effort was spent moving scaffold towers and access planks, which gave less than ideal access to work areas and also imperfect protection while working. Happily, no accident occurred, but Alister did have to put in significant extra effort to complete the roof.

It was notable that when it came time to install the solar panels, the first thing that the panel contractor did was to install a perimeter access platform with full edge protection!

▲ Completed installation of roof breather membrane.

Installing a breather membrane

The next step in the roof construction was to install a breather membrane on top of the rafters. This membrane, made of polyester fibres, is impermeable to liquid water but will allow water vapour to pass through. The purpose of the membrane is to stop any water that somehow is driven through the tiles from entering the building. It also helps to reduce draughts in the building as the structure will be open to the roof, and at this stage is not intended to be insulated.

Tiling the roof

The tiling strategy changed a couple of times before it actually started. At first, reclaimed tiles were to be bought and a steel liner tray was to be used under the solar panels on the south side of the roof. The cost of buying tiles was more than the cost of the steel liner, so this made economic sense and would have saved a fair amount of work.

However, Alister was offered some free tiles from a

▲ Tiles from demolition project stacked for re-use.

◄ Cleaning the tiles prior to use was dirty work.

demolition project. This meant that he didn't have to buy any tiles or a steel liner. It was a fair amount of extra work to recover, transport, clean and then install all of those extra tiles but the money saved on this part of the job (and construction materials saved from landfill) could be spent on other parts of the job that were much more visible, such as quality windows and doors.

After the breathable membrane was fixed over the whole roof, a batten was fixed to the top surface of each rafter. Counter battens were fixed at right angles to these at 100mm centres up the roof to support the tiles. Fixing the battens in this way, battens and counter battens, means that there is an air gap between the underside of the tiles and the membrane so that any water getting through the tiles can easily flow down the roof and is directed away from the building at the eaves.

Another point to note is the three-quarter-length tile at the very bottom of the roof and the double thickness of the lowest batten to lift the bottom edge of this tile so that the one above 'sits' at the correct level.

The battens were fixed to the sweet chestnut rafters with stainless-steel screws, whereas the counter battens were fixed to the battens with galvanised nails (as mentioned previously, galvanising is suitable for damp environments but doesn't have the same degree of protection against the acids in sweet chestnut as stainless steel).

The tiles were fixed to the battens with galvanised nails. Only every third or so tile was held in place with nails. In contrast to the sweet chestnut shakes on the 8 x 6 Shed (see page 101), the self weight of the concrete tiles holds them in place. If one becomes cracked, due to impact or frost, then it is easier to replace a broken tile or area of tiles if only a small proportion are fully fixed. The rest of the tiles are held in place by the tags on the back of the tile, their own self weight and the weight of other tiles around them.

Once the battens were fixed and the bottom couple of rows of tiles in place, it was a matter of working away cleaning and fixing tiles until the job was done. Alister did this work

▶ Tiling continuing from the bottom corner in an orderly and systematic manner.

▼ Close-up of completed bottom section of roof. Note the even spacing of the tiles, especially the bottom row.

alongside his day job during evenings, weekends and a couple of bank holidays. We think you'll agree that the final result looks very good.

With the roof just about in place, it was time to give the solar panel installer a call to firm up on the installation date.

▶ The starter row of tiles, so important to get this bit right.

▼ The south face of the roof with 80% of the tiles installed. Stockpile of tiles in the bottom right of the picture.

5. Adding the solar panels

The solar panel installation was undertaken by a specialist supplier/installer – Joju Solar Ltd. The company was selected on the basis of its reputation and long standing through the ups and downs of the solar industry.

The installation was actually undertaken by two separate specialists, Joju Solar Ltd and a local electrician who installed

▼ Clips fixing support frames to rafters.

the fusebox in the shed to which the output of the solar panels was connected.

Joju Solar and their team of scaffolders erected an access scaffold around the south side of the roof. This created safe working access to everywhere that was needed.

Next to be involved were the roofers. They fixed a proprietary support frame to the rafters using clips that were slid underneath the tiles and screwed to the rafters beneath. The panels were fixed to the frame. Ten panels comprising 96 individual mini cells were installed.

With the panels installed and tested, the Joju Solar electrician completed commissioning of the installation by connecting the output of the inverter to Alister's meter and undertaking commissioning checks.

The electricity thus generated is then fed through an isolating switch into the fusebox for the shed and back to Alister's electricity meter. A monitor on the control box rack shows the power being generated. At the time we were there it was a hot, sunny, summer's day and the system was generating 3kW, which seems to be a pretty good output. This will, of course, reduce on cloudy days and during the winter. On a less than stunning day in September, we noted the output of the system at 1kW.

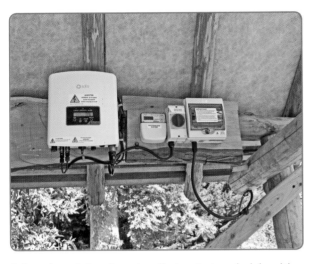

▲ Control panels for solar system. The inverter is on the left and the fuse box is on the right.

▲ Close-up of power monitor showing 3010W.

Solar panel efficiency

The efficiency of solar panels has increased dramatically since the early 2000s when residential solar electric installations first started. The panels supplied to this project provide almost three times the output per square metre than panels installed in the early days.

The panels generate a constant 12V direct current (DC) electricity – this is converted to the 240V alternating current that is used in a domestic supply using an inverter. This changes the voltage and signal to a sine wave that can be used by any domestic appliance. The panels are durable and come with a 25-year guarantee.

After doing his sums, Alister calculated that the £7,000 cost of installing the panels would be recovered over 12 to 15 years, depending on the final efficiency of the system. And over the projected lifetime of the panels, the investment would return the equivalent of 7% per year.

Solar power has indeed come a long way from the early days when it was seen very much as a novelty. This system receives some small subsidy for generating 'green power' and reducing carbon emissions. On a more personal level, it reduces Alister's electricity bills and enables him to charge his all-electric Nissan Leaf car at minimal cost.

▼ View of solar panel installation on south-facing roof slope.

6. Installing the floor

Up until this point, all of the build focus had been on the roof. The reason for this was that the frame structure was stable without the walls and floor. Moreover, completing the roof as soon as possible in the spring/summer would mean a dry space underneath where construction of the floor and walls could be completed, regardless of the weather outside.

Completing the floor structure

The floor of the shed was supported on the same foundation pads as the frame by 6 x 4 timbers spanning 3.5m between the pads. The floor was then formed using 6 x 2 C24 joists spanning 2.7m at 400mm centres between these floor beams. The joists were supported off the floor beams using joist hangers fixed with 30mm-long wire twist nails.

Joist hangers aren't a new invention by any means. They save a huge amount of work in contrast to the traditional practice of notching floor joists into floor beams.

The design of the floor incorporated a double joist around the perimeter of the shed, which took account of the curved posts and enabled support for the perimeter walls.

Timber blocks (noggins) were nailed between the joists at the third points of the joist spans. The purpose of these blocks is to transfer load from one joist to adjoining joists.

▲ View of frame and foundations before starting floor construction.

This load sharing reduces 'bounce' in the floor and makes it feel much more solid. When nailing the noggins in place, two nails are used in each side to prevent them rotating.

Noggins are also normally staggered so that you can access the nails to the end of each noggin for hammering. In the picture, the noggins aren't alternately staggered due to the main floor beams not being parallel. Noggins were cut from the offcuts from the floor joists, which were ordered as

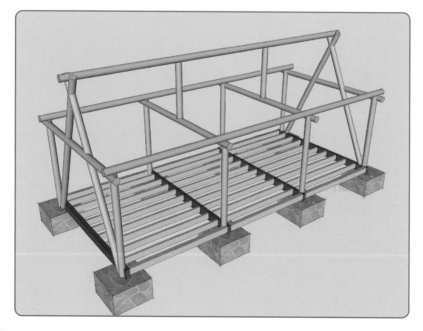

◀ General arrangement showing floor structure and pad foundations.

▼ View of joist hangers used to support the floor joists off the floor beams.

standard lengths but inevitably had short offcut lengths to
suit site dimensions.

▲ Floor structure in place.

▼ Floor sheets of OSB on the floor structure prior to fitting.

Installing the floor decking

With the floor structure complete, the floor decking could
be installed. We used 18mm-thick OSB for the floor decking.

In many sheds, the floor deck doubles up as the floor. This is
because many sheds are fairly utilitarian and there is no need to
go to the extra expense of having both a floor deck and
flooring. For other buildings, a separate floor covering is used to
improve the appearance and ease of cleaning. For this project, a
floor deck was used and a separate floor covering, possibly of
engineered oak flooring, was to be installed at a later date.

Standard sheets of 8 x 4ft were used and cut to size where
they interfaced with the frame columns and where the
opposing walls were not quite parallel. A handheld circular
saw was used for the long straight cuts and a smaller electric
jig saw was used for the shorter curved cuts around the posts.

As square-edged boards were used, additional noggins
were needed at the interface between boards to support
board edges and keep the floor 'solid'.

Having the floor in place made a huge difference to the 'feel'
of the shed. Before installation, moving from one end to the
other meant carefully stepping over obstructions and avoiding
obstacles. With the level floor in place, it was a pleasure to easily
walk from one end of the building to the other.

▼ OSB 'notched out' around the support posts.

For further details of the rest of the build...

We leave the project at this point with the frame
manufactured and erected, the roof weathertight, the solar
panels generating electricity and a smooth structural floor
deck in place. The completion of the project is covered on
secrets-of-shed-building.com with updates on
shedworking.co.uk

FINISHING A SHED

153

Electricity

However you want to use your shed, but especially if you are considering using it as a garden office or studio, it is well worth considering installing electrics for heating, lighting and power. Ideally, you need to consider this *before* you start your build, as it becomes a bit trickier once everything else is done.

Wiring a shed is a major undertaking and, unless you are a professional electrician, you should not attempt to do this yourself – a poorly-executed DIY job is a major health hazard for you and your family, not to mention that uncertified electrical work can land you a fine of up to £5,000.

Consider what you want to run off the supply and how many sockets you require (probably a couple more than you think you need). So, as well as considering where you'd like plugs to go, do you want just lighting and a kettle, or also a television, fridge, burglar alarm and heater? Depending on what you want, your fuse box may need upgrading.

The usual way of getting power from the house to the shed is via an armoured cable, which is buried underground,

covered with a warning tape, then backfilled with earth. The more items you need to power and the further the distance from the house, the fatter the cables need to be.

It's also important to choose a good electrician. The National Inspection Council for Electrical Installation Contracting (NICEIC) helps you search for accredited electricians locally, as does the National Association of Professional Inspectors & Testers (NAPIT) and Which? Trusted Traders. At the very least, they need to be Part P approved. Have nothing to do with them if they recommend anything like suspending cables in the air or ignoring certification to save money.

What you can safely do is dig the trench for the armoured cable yourself – it needs to be at least 600mm deep to avoid a spade accidentally going into it – so when you get a quote, mention that you are prepared to undertake this yourself (be warned though, it's a lot of work and you might need a petrol-driven trenching tool).

After the job is completed make sure you receive a Certificate of Work. This is especially important if/when you come to sell your house.

▼ A carbon neutral, cork-clad workspace with a sedum roof used by a musician and textile artist. (Cuprinol Shed of the Year)

Eco energy

▲ Going off grid is increasingly popular.

One alternative to conventional power issues is to generate your own electricity. Going off-grid can mean zero running costs for light, tools and appliances, as well as cutting out the need to lay cables and dig up lawns. Kevin Holland, Managing Director of Solar Shed (www.thesolarshed.co.uk) says the key concept is to KYSS, or Keep Your Solar Simple.

'A solar panel connected to a regulator will keep a battery topped up for when you need energy,' he explains. 'It's a 20-minute job to fix a panel onto a shed roof and run the positive and negative wires from the panel down into the regulator and then two wires from the regulator into a battery. And that is all a solar system comprises of, for the purpose of powering a shed. A panel, a regulator and a battery.

'Solar power on an allotment or garden shed means light, it means you can charge batteries to power tools and run 12V appliances such as fans, or charge anything via USB ports. Once the solar, regulator and battery are in place, the 12V circuit, lighting and using an inverter can become a hobby in itself for many. A solar system can grow with your needs and requirements as they develop.'

Although most people just want a few lights and some USB-charging capability, Kevin has seen a full range of solar installations in sheds, from a simple £50 solar-powered light that comes on when you enter the shed and goes off ten minutes later to people who have retired, spend ten hours a day down the shed and have spent £2,000 or more to ensure lathes and milling machines can operate.

'Prices really do depend on your needs,' he says. 'A good 32W panel, 20A regulator and a 100ah AGM battery should cost just under £400. This would be ideal for the weekend shedworker and occasional evening shed session. For someone who will be using more power during the day then 200W of solar, a 40A regulator and 200–400ah of AGM battery will take you to over £1,200. Adding inverters to ensure appliances or chargers work will cost more, as will the lights and 12V circuits and any monitoring or automation. Being mainly 12V systems, you do not need to be an electrician. If you can wire a plug, you can wire solar.'

An additional aid to eco-friendly power is a wind generator. They come in two types, roof-mounted (cheaper) or on a freestanding pole (more efficient). One major benefit is that while they can be used all year, they are particularly successful in autumn and winter when lighting is most required. However, not all locations are suitable, especially those in sheltered and urban areas where airflow or other obstructions are an issue. Most turbines for domestic use do not need planning permission, but as ever, it's still a good idea to have a word with your local council and your neighbours before installing anything, as they can sometimes be a bit noisy.

Water

Adding a toilet, or indeed some kind of shower room, to garden buildings has become increasingly popular over the last few years and specialised suppliers are available to provide all the knowhow (at a price...). As with electricity, it's wisest to get a professional in if you want running water in your shed as there are key issues to consider such as burying pipes underground, insulation and distance from electrical cables, as well as how to remove waste water (as you're in the garden, one possibility could be a soakaway). Another major consideration is that you will have to jump through building regulation hoops and maybe even require planning permission.

If you just want a toilet, consider going down an alternative route. The Little House Company, for example, sells a range of waterless urine separators/diverters, composting toilets and other accessories (including solar panel kits) and is an official reseller for Kildwick and Separett compost toilets. The company also makes its own model, the Eco-Loo, which comes in two bespoke varieties, the 'Divert' (urine is diverted to a soakaway pit/external container) and the 'Capture' (using a built-in tank which can be completely self-contained).

▼ A composting toilet in a bothy in the Cairngorns, Scotland.

Furnishing and decoration

Once you've built your shed, it's time to think about its interior and exterior appearance. The possibilities are limitless, whether you want a man cave, a she shed, or something that's entirely unique and personal to you. You can arguably be braver about what you do with decorating your shed than decorating your sitting room.

'The increasing use of sheds as artists' studios, craft workshops, summerhouses, home offices, writing spaces or yoga studios as well as traditional workshops has come with an interest in what the building actually looks like,' says Jane Field-Lewis (www.jane-field.co.uk), author of the books *my cool shed* and *The Anatomy of Sheds*, as well as a consultant stylist for *George Clarke's Amazing Spaces* television series. 'In these cases the shed is more of an expression of an interest or a person and a space in which we spend time, rather than simply as a repository.

'The trend is to use this as an opportunity to design and decorate this new space in the same way that you decorate your home. You think about creating an interior and exterior that is pleasing to you, one that establishes an atmosphere in which you feel happy and comfortable.'

▼ The beauty of having your own shed is that you can decorate it however you like. (Cuprinol Shed of the Year)

▲ The interior of a shepherd's hut made by Dorset-based specialists Plankbridge.

One of her favourite kit-outs was a build in Nashville, a renovation of a wrecked American Shasta trailer into a stylish backyard bedroom/holiday rental. 'Its owner, with limited DIY skills and funds, transformed the interior with pine timber and with a lot of white paint, and figured out how to make his own curtains.'

Naturally Jane has thought in depth about her own shed.

'I am in the process of getting a new shed built at home. It is a simple structure, with the decoration primarily in the limited use of materials and finishes. Architectural in style, it has just three materials: a large double-glazed gable end wall, a black wooden exterior and a CNC milled plywood interior. It has to hold the garden tools, be a simple bike repair station, and be somewhere for hanging out during summer days. Although necessarily small, one entire wall swings open onto the garden to make it a less-enclosed space. It's well insulated, and the tools are hidden away in a large cupboard. I intend to put some art on the walls so that when summer is here and the wall/door is swung open, it's an attractive feature (along with the wine fridge tucked away in there too).'

Jane's top five shed decoration tips

1. **I'm a big fan of painting sheds and fences black in a garden. Contrary to instinct, it makes a space look bigger, and green plants look more striking against it.**
2. **I like a shed to look out into the garden as a whole – it makes it easier to feel like you are in a different space and helps the mind feel relaxed. So think about the position of the door and any windows, and where you are going to sit or work in there.**
3. **If there is the space available and local regulations allow, a wood-burning stove can create a wonderful atmosphere.**
4. **I've noticed that if there is a simplicity to the decorating of the space that encourages a more contemplative way of thinking, especially if you use items that mean something to you rather than simply bought.**
5. **Inspired use of materials can create an amazing structure. For example, in** *The Anatomy of Sheds* **there's an artist studio in Scotland designed by Studio Weave where the entire exterior is covered with panels of cold-pressed zinc.**

Green roofs

One of the ways you can ensure your shed looks good and also helps the environment is to add a green roof and turn it into a mini patch of garden.

Green roofs are normal roofs simply covered in some kind of vegetation on top of a special membrane or frame. The most popular type are sedum roofs, often described as a 'living carpet': sedums are small plants with chubby leaves and stems and they don't mind the rotten growing conditions of a roof. You can plant a sedum roof – either in blanket or plug format – almost anywhere, but your roof does need to be quite strong, since after a downpour it can become very heavy indeed, and be pretty flat (not more than about 20 degrees is a general rule of thumb).

There are numerous benefits. Happily they are inexpensive, look attractive and also provide good insulation – cooler inside in summer, warmer in winter – as well as absorbing air pollution and reducing noise levels (you'll also lose that 'drumming' sound when it rains). They also look good pretty much from day one and distract the eye from more conventional darker roofs with naturally-changing greens and reds.

Although they're hardy, a sedum roof needs plenty of sunlight. **Sedum roofs are low rather than no maintenance, so you will have to keep an eye on it and weed/fertilise two or three times a year**. You also need to get rid of bits of twig or fallen leaves and any other debris. And while it doesn't need much water, when it's as hot as the summer of 2018, then it will need a helping hand.

If you're really keen, then you can go a stage further and effectively turn your shed roof into an allotment. You'll need to talk to an expert first about how strong your roof needs to be to hold the extra weight, whatever kind of green roof you go for, but one which you farm obviously needs even more thought (I've even come across one on which goats graze!).

One of the best examples is Joel Bird's urban pride and joy and a past winner of the Shed of the Year competition in 2014. The main part of the shed is used as a workshop, painting studio and music room. Up above are peas, beetroot, carrots, strawberries and much, much more fruit and veg. A small staircase provides access to the roof.

Many of the leading garden room suppliers can supply a green roof with your new building. Green Roof Shelters are experts at turning shipping containers into garden offices and other shedlike buildings such as cycle stores and outdoor classrooms. They can also advise on habitat walls that encourage bees, bats and other wildlife.

If you like the idea of a green roof but want something even lower maintenance, consider an artificial grass roof, which not only looks good year-round but also requires no planning permission, unlike sedum or wildflower ones which usually do because of the roofing work required. You do still need to think about rainwater run-off and drainage too. And while it's mainly green, other colours are available, such as the Wimbledon from LazyLawn, which is more purple but with flecks of green. Some sheddies like the artificial version so much that they even use it as carpet inside the shed…

▼ Green roofs are attractive and environmentally friendly. (Rotunda Roundhouses)

SHEDLIKE STRUCTURES

Garden offices

Garden offices are one of the most popular reinventions of the shed concept in the last 20 years. These, often remarkably high-tech, structures at the end of the back garden are bringing back the idea of the cottage industry and renewing the strong connection between work life and home life. Technology is now helping to set the workforce free.

Famous shedworkers who have attracted the most attention are artists and writers such as George Bernard Shaw, Roald Dahl, Henry Thoreau and Henry Moore. But, nowadays, you're just as likely to find accountants at the bottom of the garden as you are sculptors. And while men's interest in some kind of shedlike manspace remains unshakeable, over the last few years women have been quietly redefining shedlife, turning the new breed of garden buildings into places to work, to create and to think, as well as to hang the secateurs.

There are many advantages to turning your shed into a workspace. A major consideration is the ten-second commute, compared to the lengthy and expensive journey by car or public transport. The great thing about a garden office is that it marks a clear difference between where you live and where you work, yet it also involves going somewhere to begin your working day which is important, a kind of ceremony. Physically, it's easier to prevent – or at least restrict – your children, spouse and pets invading your workspace if you're based in a garden office. Also, by using a shed, your third bedroom or dining room table remains free from a deluge of wires and paper. Financially, it adds value to your property, up to 5% according to some estate agents' reports.

There are now many companies offering off-the-peg garden offices, but if you can build a shed, you can certainly build yourself a garden office too. If you don't want to build it from scratch, one option is to use a kit from a supplier, adding your key elements such as insulation, decking, additional storage space, etc.

◄ A simple garden office can be the perfect place to work.

Shepherds' huts

Former Prime Minister David Cameron is the latest in a long line of well-known owners of a shepherd's hut, including naturalist Kate Humble, Gabriel Oak in Thomas Hardy's novel *Far From the Madding Crowd* and actress Helena Bonham-Carter's daughter, whose bedroom was a shepherd's hut. And it's not hard to see why the shepherd's hut industry is booming – no longer a working man's modest temporary accommodation on wheels, they have become as popular as garden offices, workshops and glamping retreats. Mr Cameron plans to use his to pen his political memoirs, although his children want to requisition it as more of a rumpus room.

'It simply gives me somewhere to write in the middle of what I do,' says Mark Diacono, founder of Otter Farm near Honiton in Devon (www.otterfarm.co.uk), 'somewhere I do no admin, which is just dedicated to writing, something very important for one so easily distracted as I. There are many reasons why I chose a shepherd's hut – in no particular order: cheapness, no planning needed, mobile, and the space just suited me perfectly. I couldn't be happier with mine.'

Mr Cameron's pride and joy, made by Red Sky Shepherd's Huts, is fairly typical – it measures 16 x 7ft, has an arched roof, metal wheels and a wood-burning stove. But there is a tremendous variety out there. Blackdown Shepherd Huts, for example, offer solar power add-ons, as well as a self-build option. Even the size is controversial, with Richard Lee of Dorset-based Plankbridge particularly keen on the traditional 12 x 6ft size, the right dimensions to ensure they can pass smoothly through farm gates. He regards some of the modern builds on the market as 'timber-clad carbuncles'. (Indeed, Eddie Grundy had similar reservations when Lynda first mentioned her intention to buy, arguing that some models appeared to 'mock the working man's heritage'.)

Dave Morris thinks along similar lines. Dave is author of the excellent *Shepherds' Huts & Living Vans*, the best book on the subject, which also clarifies the difference between these and other similar huts (such as road roller huts and steam threshing crew huts), describing not only how they differ in design, but also how they were used by their occupants on a daily basis. 'We all enjoy our huts today, mostly recreationally,' he says, 'but I think it is important not

▲ The shepherd's hut has made a strong comeback in the last ten years. (Plankbridge)

to forget that these were once people's real workplaces and often operating in very tough conditions on the knife edge of financial success or failure.'

One of the best places to see shepherds' huts in action is at the regular Shepherding & Shepherds' Huts event held every year around April at the Weald and Downland Living Museum, West Dean, near Chichester. There are shepherd-related activities such as folk singing and gate hurdle making, as well as the museum's fascinating collection of historic huts and living vans. In addition, manufacturers usually showcase their current models.

'The shepherd's hut offers a traditional, quirky option among the fairly broad choice of garden buildings,' says Richard Lee, who set up Plankbridge (www.plankbridge.com) a decade ago with Jane Dennison. 'They tap into childhood stories, a romantic retreat away from the stresses of the world. Cast iron wheels suggest escape, freedom.'

Beach huts

Wherever you look, these iconic buildings dominate the British landscape (as well as architecture firm Scott Brownrigg's design for the London office of Google). You'll increasingly find them everywhere from RHS Flower Shows to the annual beach hut advent calendar in Brighton and Hove.

There are around 20,000 beach huts around the coast, descendants of the bathing machine, their sheds-on-wheels ancestors and a 19th century must-have for a trip to the seaside in France, Germany and America, as well as Britain. Back then, men's machines were placed some distance away from women's, although built on similar lines: wooden frames, 6 x 8ft with a shedlike roof, either painted or covered in adverts. Each had a front and back door, about 4ft off the ground. Nowadays, not only the etiquette but the architecture has moved on, as exemplified in the Bathing Beauties project.

Bathing Beauties was an international competition set up in 2006 that featured hundreds of cutting-edge designs and models by artists and architects who took the British beach hut as their starting point and then gave the concept a wash and brush up, such as the enormous two-storey gin and

tonic-shaped hut. The winners of the competition were rewarded with a commission to build their designs on the Lincolnshire coast along a ten-mile stretch of coast between Mablethorpe and Chapel St. Leonards. Bathing Beauties turned into a travelling exhibition and is now an annual arts and crafts festival.

'We deal with huts from Scotland, down to the Isle of Wight, with lots in the middle,' says Matt Briggs of specialist insurer, Love Your Hut. 'Most of them tend to be of wood construction, but some are brick, some are concrete and some of the newer huts are now being made of composite materials, which are more resistant to our coastal weather.'

Whatever they are made of, beach huts are big business in the 21st century. Prices have risen so fast over the last decade that the most expensive beach huts are nudging the £300,000 mark. In terms of property investment alone, it appears that at the moment you can't go wrong.

And if that's too much, simply sit back and read a good book about beach huts. The best is by architectural historian and beach hut specialist, Kathryn Ferry. Her marvellous *Sheds on the Seashore: A Tour Through Beach Hut History* is a very readable and excellently researched trip from the beginnings of the beach hut through to its present day renaissance.

▼ Beach huts are top of many seaside visitors' must-have lists. (Love Your Hut)

Rotating sheds

There's only one thing better than a shed, and that's a shed that moves. Shepherds' huts provide one option for those who want to manoeuvre their pride and joy at will, and many of the new breed of tiny homes are built on trailers specificially so they can be transported. And, of course, you can also go down the self-build route. Kevin Nicks' VW Passat-based motorised shed, often seen on the country's roads raising money for charity, has been officially clocked at speeds just shy of 100mph.

But most shed owners are not looking for quite this level of mobility; something more sedate is the order of the day, something which won't make you spill your tea. And this is why, for over a century, sheds that slowly rotate have carved out their own little niche in the shed world.

Sculptor Henry Moore had a rather nice one at his Hoglands home in Hertfordshire (sadly it's now static), and followers of the Shed of the Year competition will remember Bryan Lewis Jones's revolving masterpiece, which won the Unique category in the 2016 Shed of the Year awards, narrowly missing out on scooping the top overall prize.

But the most famous by far is the one owned by

playwright and general all-round egghead George Bernard Shaw, see page 11, who was inspired by his friend and neighbour, the naturalist explorer Apsley Cherry-Garrard, who had a revolving shelter in the grounds of his house nearby. Shaw wrote *Pygmalion* and *Major Barbara* in his hut at his home in Shaw's Corner, Ayot St Lawrence, near St Albans. Built in 1906 by Stawson's, this had a revolving base, which used a series of castors mounted on a circular track. This meant it could be adjusted via a lever to improve the light inside as well as to change the view (or indeed just for some mild exercise).

One of the aspects of the Lazy Susan-style that attracted Shaw was its potential for improving health. In the early 20th century the likes of Henry & Julius Caesar and Norwich-based Boulton & Paul were the titans of the summerhouse industry and made revolving models based on small Alpine chalets in Swiss tuberculosis sanitoriums. Here, TB sufferers (Shaw lost two siblings to the disease in early life) benefited from the constant flow of fresh air, as well as ready access to sunshine. These were for use in private gardens as well as hospitals in the UK, with large windows and paintwork reminiscent of muted beach hut colours. Today, examples in a decent state of repair in salvage yards usually cost around £10,000.

▼ A Boulton and Paul rotating summerhouse restored by The Fourpenny Workshop.

Tiny houses

The age of the tiny house is coming. (Tiny House UK)

Our homes are getting smaller. The average British house has shrunk by two square metres in the past decade and the UK now has the smallest new build homes in Western Europe. While the government soundbites off vaguely about the benefits of 'high-quality compact living models', shedlike structures are one solution to the problem.

Over the last few years, the idea that we can be just as happy living in a (much) smaller home has been gaining ground in the USA and there is now growing acceptance of the values of the tiny house movement over here in the UK. Advocates argue that living small is not only more affordable but offers an ecologically friendly alternative. These homes – generally defined as under 400 square feet – also make the best possible use of the transformer furniture trend, with chairs and sofas turning into tables and beds and storage space cleverly built in to the most unexpected places.

Leading the way on this side of the pond is Mark Burton from Tiny House UK who has now put together a special Tiny House Kit for the growing numbers of people who want to build their own titchy home. From the outside, they do have a slightly shedlike appearance but inside they are extremely comfortable and boast all the normal domestic appliances with composting WC and kitchen units as extras. They're warm, cheap – coming in at a starting price of £6,500 – and can be built on wheels, so moving house is really rather easy.

'It's a concept that is really striking a chord in all age groups, but especially in the younger generation,' says Mark. 'I now receive hundreds of emails monthly from people wanting to buy, build or rent a tiny home to live in.'

The latest entry into the micro living market is Zedbox, a design which comes from Smart Garden Offices.

'Creating a building that we can manufacture in component form, that's desirable, pretty, robust, moveable, affordable and conforms with building regulations in both England and Scotland is very complicated,' says Smart's managing director, Charlie Dalton, who has been building garden offices for decades.

'As a child I was always designing small house layouts, and have always been intrigued by real home ergonomics. Now as a 50-year-old, I still feel it's my calling. Since 2001, I've been asked on a regular basis "can I live in this?" about my garden offices, so I've always known there'll be substantial demand for a properly specified MicroHouse.'

Charlie estimates that within five years, between 35,000 and 50,000 'micro homes' will be built each year.

So where will all these owners of tiny houses live? 'When planning laws are changed to free up unused council-owned and agricultural land, that will make it possible to obtain planning permission for small dwellings, and then the micro home/tiny house lifestyle will skyrocket,' says Mark. 'Farmers would greet this trend with open arms and would gladly designate a corner of land if they could benefit from some rent.'

Charlie Dalton agrees that regulations are at the heart of the future of the tiny house movement.

'The real impact on creating homes, in volume, for the next generation will come about not by large-scale, long-term building projects and new towns but by increasing the density of the existing house stock, quickly, cheaply, sustainably and subtly. If only the regulations about permitted development rights could be improved…'

Round sheds

Of course, not all sheds have to be variations on a box. In recent years there has been a trend towards a more rounded look. The spherical Pod from York-based Archipod (www. archipod.com) is an insulated, prefab, curved plywood shedlike space roughly 3m in diameter and with a height of 2.5m from floor to underside of the rooflight. Or for those who like their shedworking more elliptical, the Escape Pod from Podmakers (www. podmakers.co.uk) is run by furniture maker Dominic Ash and treehouse engineer specialist Jeremy Fitter. It's made out of birch ply and oak then clad in cedar shingles and, best of all, can be rotated like George Bernard Shaw's classic garden office, as it is built onto a Lazy Susan-type platform 50cm off the ground.

'We serve to illustrate that modular buildings needn't be boring,' says Gemma Roe, founder and spatial designer at the decidedly rounded Rotunda Roundhouses (rotunda.co.uk).

'From an environmental perspective, circular buildings require fewer resources compared to a rectilinear structure of the same floor area, due to the simple fact that a circle encloses the largest area for a given amount of perimeter, saving about 30%. Given that the planet is being depleted of resources at

an astonishing rate, felling trees to build corners for the sake of it seems illogical to us. This, in turn also makes it the most energy efficient form we could design, given that the external surface area is greatly reduced, thus reducing energy depletion. Furthermore, the internal space promotes fantastic thermal dynamics, warm air rotates upwards and drops down in a central column beneath the cool roof light dome, independently circulating and maintaining its temperature.'

Of course, there's also the aesthetic element too – exterior curves and circles simply fit well into the natural world, and the interiors of a rotunda are lovely too, with exposed timber beams leading to a double-glazed rooflight dome.

'On a psychological level, circular spaces are hard wired into our DNA since our ancient ancestors commonly resided in roundhouses,' says Gemma. 'As a social or workshop space, the circular form is ideal for group work or gatherings. This is especially crucial when building for schools and inspiring young children.' As well as garden offices and classrooms, the company also provides buildings for luxury glamping sites and yoga retreats.

▲ Round sheds make an intriguing contrast to the traditional shape. (Rotunda Roundhouses)

SHED CULTURE

Shed of the Year

Although sheds have always been with us, their public profile has risen astonishingly in the last decade. And that's largely thanks to Andrew Wilcox and his Shed of the Year competition.

'I have run the readersheds.co.uk website about sheds since 2001,' explains Andrew, a freelance web designer, better known in the sheddie world as Uncle Wilco. 'It started as a bit of fun but it got popular very quickly and the idea of a National Shed Week and a Shed of the Year competition came to me in 2006. Before then, there was nothing out there to celebrate the great British shed. So in 2007 we made our first award – the inaugural winner was a Roman temple shed. I thought we could not top that, but each year the sheddies amaze me.'

The mainstream media initially treated it as something of a joke, if indeed they covered it at all. Fast forward a decade and now every national newspaper and major website runs galleries of the shortlisted entrants and finalists in August, it has a major sponsor in the form of Cuprinol, and has spawned an annual series on television fronted by George Clarke, which highlights the more unusual and inventive entries. When episodes are aired, Twitter goes crazy (often with the complaint, 'that's not a shed!' when a particularly complex build is shown).

There's an incredible range of shed builds, including pubs, cinemas, churches and pirate ships, as well as more conventional structures. And it has certainly struck a chord with the public. In 2017, there were nearly 3,000 entries and more than 12,000 public votes in the first stage of the contest. The winner, a popular choice, was the 'West Wing' from Berkshire, made almost entirely from recycled materials and containing a hidden room behind a secret bookcase.

'Everyone loves a shed,' says Andrew, 'but I did not realise the lengths people go to when they start creating their own spaces. Sheds are no longer just storage areas for your garden tools, they're now a part of people's everyday lives.' Indeed, they are. According to figures from Cuprinol, around two-thirds of people in Britain now own a shed, with those under 25 slightly more likely to have one than people aged 45 to 54, and increasingly likely to use it as a yoga room or garden office rather than simply as a place to keep the lawnmower.

Diplomatically, Uncle Wilco is reluctant to name a favourite shed and is obviously as keen on the simple traditional shed found on allotments as the high-tech ones that rotate or are built on various levels. 'They are all amazing. The sheddies are a great community of people with a love of garden buildings. But the winner from 2013 – the Boat Roofed shed – is the one I have revisited a few years after it won the competition. It's in a great spot on top of a mountain in Mid Wales and the sheddies who built it have become good friends.'

◀ The Roman temple shed, the first winner of the Shed of the Year competition. (readersheds.co.uk)

▶ The Viking Hutte, winner of the 2018 Shed of the Year workshop category. Note the shingles. (Cuprinol Shed of the Year)

Men's Sheds Association

The traditional function of a shed is to provide a refuge, somewhere to get well away from the world at large. But a hugely successful new initiative is helping some people to do exactly the opposite.

The Men's Sheds movement was established in Australia in 2006 to provide local venues in which men (often of retirement age) could meet, socialise and work on practical tasks on a regular basis with other local men. Since then, the concept has caught on elsewhere and the first Men's Shed opened in England in 2009 – the latest figures from the UK Men's Sheds Association shows more than 450 are now active. Among organisations that have got behind the schemes are Age UK, which helped organise the first EiSHEDfod in Wales, and the Royal Voluntary Service, which has established a Sheds Grant Fund to finance community 'Shed' spaces. Alzheimer's Support has just started working with the Brunel Shed in Corsham.

There is no age limit to Shed membership, although most men are in the 50+ age group and lack networks of close friends. Activities are usually hands-on physical pursuits such as woodworking, metal working and general repairs, but rather than doing them alone in the back garden, men work with others with whom they can share skills, companionship

▼ The purpose-built Repair Shed in Hemel Hempstead for the local Men's Shed group. (Chris Lee)

and really rotten jokes. A Shed is also a safe place to talk about concerns about jobs, divorce, family and health. Sessions tend to be held during the day, funded through a variety of measures including grants and small individual session charges.

A 2016 study by Steven Markham, Lecturer and Researcher in the School of Health and Community Studies at Leeds Beckett University, found not only were Sheds helpful in reducing isolation and loneliness, but that men Shedders felt more connected to their local communities and had a greater sense of purpose. They enjoyed being with and wanted to help other people.

'This is a key point,' says Steven, 'because men often do not want to be the recipients of "services". Through the Men's Shed, the men were given an avenue, the resources and encouragement to be able to help others. By doing so, this increased their confidence and sense of self-worth and improved their well-being.'

Chris Lee, a UK Men's Sheds Trustee who helped set up The Repair Shed in Hemel Hempstead (www.facebook.com/TheRepairShed), describes these sheds as 'communal work-and-play spaces', not always actual sheds, sometimes just rooms in a community centre, sports pavilion, empty garage and, in one case, a disused mortuary.

'Everybody gets different things from the weekly dose of fun and friendship,' he says. 'Unemployed "Shedders", as we call ourselves, may have low confidence. One guy took

▲ Men's Sheds provide a sociable space to enjoy hobbies.

about six months to "find his voice" and another got a job after being long-term unemployed – a loss to the Shed but an "occupational hazard"! Another guy was getting over the death of his partner and didn't feel he had anything to contribute – we reassured him that didn't matter and he buddied up with one of the guys and learnt lots in an unpressured way.

'Some of the guys "put in more than they take out" and get the buzz of seeing people blossom around them through purposeful activity. But ultimately tea, chairs, a table and a sense of humour are the most important ingredients for a successful Men's Shed. We do know that Sheds have stopped men killing themselves.'

Find your nearest Shed at: www.menssheds.org.uk/find-a-shed.

Chris's tips for setting up a Men's Shed

- ■ Aim for sustainability from the start, with a small group planning and developing the Shed around their particular skills and interests
- ■ Involve women in recruiting 'Shedders' because women usually 'get' the Shed concept before men. Women can also be Men's Shed members
- ■ Premises are key – make sure you have a suitable space with access that suits your members in terms of times, is handy for public transport and is suitable for people with disabilities. It's usually best to try to find space in an existing organisation's premises and then look for somewhere bigger if you need more space.

Bibliography

George Clarke and Jane Field-Lewis, *George Clarke's Amazing Spaces* (Quadrille, 2013)

Sally Coulthard, *How to Build a Shed* (Laurence King, 2018)

Sally Coulthard, *Shed Chic* (Jacqui Small, 2009)

Sally Coulthard, *Shed Decor* (Jacqui Small, 2015)

Sally Coulthard, *Studio* (Jacqui Small, 2017)

Jane Field-Lewis, *The Anatomy of Sheds: New buildings from an old tradition* (Pavilion, 2016)

Jane Field-Lewis, *my cool shed* (Pavilion, 2012)

Alex Johnson, *Shedworking: The alternative workplace revolution* (Frances Lincoln, 2010)

David Morris, *Shepherds' Huts & Living Vans* (Amberley, 2013)

Michael Pollan, *A Place of my Own* (Delta, 1997)

Lester Walker, *Tiny Tiny Houses* (Black Dog and Leventhal, 1987)

Art Boericke, Barry Shapiro, *Handmade Houses, A Guide to the Woodbutcher's Art* (Idea Books International, 1975)

Aidan Chopra, *Google SketchUp for Dummies* (Wiley Publishing Inc, 2007)

R. Chudley and R. Greeno, *Building Construction Handbook* (Butterworth Heinemann, 2016)

Fiona Cobb, *Structural Engineer's Pocket Book* (CRC Press, 2014)

Nigel Dunnet, Dusty Gedge, John Little and Edmund C. Snodgrass, *Small Green Roofs* (Timber Press, 2011)

Ben Law, *Roundwood Timber Framing* (Permanent Publications, 2010)

WB McKay, *Carpentry* (Longmans, 1966)

Gordon Thorburn, *Men and Sheds* (New Holland, 2002)

Suppliers

Screwfix – screwfix.com

South East Oak Sawmills – southeastoaksawmills.co.uk

Secrets-of-shed-building.com

Useful contacts

Tool and hardware

■ **Screwfix Direct** – Large supplier of tools and hardware
www.screwfix.com

■ **Toolstation** - Large supplier of tools and hardware
www.toolstation.com

■ **Birkdale Sales** – Supplier of Gatemate locks
www.birkdalesales.com

■ **Kreg Tool** – Developer of the Kreg Jig and other tool systems
www.kregtool.com

■ **Roundwood timber** – supplier of oak frames and stainless steel fixings
www.roundwood.com

■ **Gas Struts**:
StrutsDepot – www.strutsdepot.com
SGS Engineering – www.sgs-engineering.com

Materials

■ **South East Oak Sawmills** – Small supplier of Oak and sweet chestnut timber
southeastoaksawmills.co.uk

■ **Woodnet** – Website to enable small time timber users to contact timber growers directly
www.woodnet.org.uk/woodlots

■ **Rubber4roofs** – EPDM supplier
www.rubber4roofs.co.uk

■ **Osmostains** – Interior and external wood finishes
www.osmouk.com

■ **Dunster house** – Supplier of log cabins
www.dunsterhouse.co.uk

■ **Joju solar Ltd** – Solar Energy, battery storage and electric vehicle charging experts
www.jojusolar.co.uk

Information and advice

■ **Secrets-of-shed-building.com** – John's website offering practical tips and advice on all aspects of building a shed

■ **Shedworking.co.uk** – Alex's blog about the lifestyle of shedworkers and those who work from garden offices and other shed-like atmospheres

■ **Ben Law** – Woodsman, author and eco-builder
www.ben-law.co.uk